AS THE TREE FELL

The History and Reunion of
Our Croatian Immigrant Family

And

The Joys and Challenges of
Retirement on Vis
An Adriatic Island

by

Patricia Repanich

Patricia Repanich
Visit my website at www.vis-villa.hr

Email: asthetreefell@vis-villa.hr

Printed in the United States of America

First Printing: May, 2011

Second revised Printing: December, 2012

ISBN- 13-978-148-1222334 10-148-1222-333

Digital Edition is available on Kindle Books

COMMENTS FROM READERS:

This will be for you a surprise letter coming from New Zealand but I have to write to say how wonderful for me to have read your book 'As The Tree Fell'

Our Grandfather was from Vis and we have no background at all about him. his name Nicholas Bradanovich Capello.

I picked up your book in the little Tourist Office in Vis so we have come home with one each and keep saying to each other what a shame we had not read it prior to going away.

So Patricia thank you for writing the book. What a marvellous achievement, it has been an inspiration for us.

Sincerely
Anne Reyes Bradanovich

Wow! I just finished reading "As the Tree Fell" (about 5 min. ago). I have to say thank you for writing this book. I am from Zagreb, Croatia. I left my country 17 years ago and I miss it so much especially around Christmas holidays. With this book you brought me so close to my country that I hated to finish reading it. I wish there are more pages to read and more pictures to show my kids.
I hope you and John are doing great and your Croatian is getting better, if not *NEMA PROBLEMA* because it will get better, just keep talking (at least we Croatians love to talk).
Marcela Harrington

We have enjoyed reading the book and it has certainly got us in the mode of looking at a trip to Vis next year. It has also got us back on the genealogy trail. There are of course some parallels between the Repanich's and the Kukura's.

Thanks again for writing your book.

Best regards,

Jeff and Jan Kukura

 I have just finished your wonderful book As The Tree Fell, which I bought in Vis town. I want to thank you for making this stay of ours on this beautiful island even more beautiful. The sweet and heartfelt story of the book really enhances My experience of this place. We are currently staying in Komiza and yesterday after a good long read on the beach I had some exquisite grilled sardines and chard.

The story of emigrants and immigrants resonates also to a Nordic fellow like myself - several of my ancestors as well as my wife's ancestors moved to America. So in our families too we have stories of relatives having moved to the new world.

Anyway, once again thank you for this wonderful book. Vis is such a lovely island.

As a lover of historical fiction, I especially enjoyed reading the letters between the American and Croatian families. The author had access to actual letters that the Croatians had saved and created believable responses to them from her interviews with the Croatian relatives. Together they paint a pictue of the life and times of ordinary people living in two different worlds from 1901 to 1955. The times were especially hard for the Croatians, and the importance of family was touching.

Anyone who plans a trip to this area or has ever done a remodel will enjoy learning about the beautiful Island of Vis and the experiences of the author and her husband as they moved to a different culture and remodeled their home.

TABLE OF CONTENTS

Chapter	Page

PART 1

BLUE-EYED WAVES

PART 2

BACK IN TIME

Chapter		Page

PART 3
THE JOYS AND CHALLENGES

PREFACE

In 1999, at retirement age (when most people are trying to simplify their lives, traveling with comfortable tours and looking for the easy life) my husband, John, and I bought a seaside house in Croatia, a nine year old fledgling democracy, formerly a part of communist Yugoslavia. We took on the challenge of integrating into a culture that has endured immeasurable hardships and terrible economies in one of the most beautiful places on earth.

While searching for John's ancestral roots, we grew to know the Repanić family that still lives on the island of Vis, the homeland of John's paternal grandmother and grandfather. The parallels between the Repanić family in the "old country" and our Repanich family in America seemed to be worthy of recording. Relatives on both sides created family trees and brought out carefully stored pictures and letters from the back rooms to share with us. The feelings about separating from their families, life in a different world and their continued caring for each other became very clear and our entry into their world very meaningful.

I have based the story on translated letters, interviews, stories and other information gleaned from my observations. I have taken the liberty to enhance them as I have come to feel events may have happened.

Below are the sounds of some commonly used Croatian letters that are different from English to help the reader pronounce the Croatian names and words:

"Č"and "Ć" sound something like "CH" in church;

"C" sounds like "TS" in cats;

"J" sounds like"Y" in yellow;

"Ž" sounds like"S" in pleasure;

"Š" sounds like"SH" in English;

"LJ" sounds like the "LLI" in million;

The Croatian custom of naming the first son after the father's father and the second son after the mother's father makes it a challenge to keep all the Antes and Josips in this family straight. They undoubtedly had nicknames to use on an everyday basis, but records show only the given name. They will each have different nicknames for our purposes.

From an American perspective, our experiences dealing with the Croatian language and culture, and especially the Vis culture, have been joyous, challenging, at times frustrating and usually humorous, but we have always thought of them as a learning experience and enjoyed every minute. It is a pleasure to share them with you, the reader.

PART ONE

BLUE-EYED WAVES

VIS HARBOR

CHAPTER 1
WHY CAN'T YOU BE NORMAL?

This is the question posed by our two adult children when we announce that we are purchasing what, to us, is an exquisite seaside villa on a beautiful, secluded island in Croatia on the Adriatic Sea. To them it sounds like a run-down, war-torn shack, halfway around the world in an unstable, unsafe foreign country. The people don't speak English and there is no nearby Costco. We have lost our minds (and probably their inheritance). What led us to Vis?

In the spring of 1999, we were planning our first European adventure using frequent flyer miles acquired when we built our ranch house on our walnut farm near Corning in northern California. They would expire soon if we didn't use them. We decided to go to Russia to visit a farmer we had met when he was on a "farmer to farmer" tour in California. He had described his Krasnodar area on the Black Sea with forests of native wild walnuts, prunes, cherries, and apples... a must see for John, who at the time was a walnut grower and very interested and involved as a grower in the research of new walnut varieties.

We set aside three days of our eighteen-day trip for a side trip to the Island of Vis in Croatia to see if we could find any of John's relatives that remained on the island. His grandfather Ivan Repanich, grandmother, Katica Lipanovich, and their nine-year-old son Anton immigrated to the USA in the early 1900's. John knew only what his deceased Uncle Anton had told him of his recollection of life on Vis before he came to Fresno. John's father, Nick, was born in Fresno and had very little interest in "the old country" since his parents told him as soon as he entered school that he was not to speak "Slav", but to fit in and be American. Family conversations about the island did not interest him as he had never known these people.

Anton and his wife, Winnie, had a few photographs of two families taken around 1949 that they had used for determining the right size clothes to send in care packages to the Croatian family. The names that went with the pictures (Josip, Dinko, Rina, Drago, Stipe, Mare, Ante, Jerina, Joško, Jozo, and Perina) sounded so foreign and intriguing. There had been no correspondence between the two families since 1955. We knew that Vis had been closed to tourists until after 1991 when Croatia won their independence from Yugoslavia in the Homeland War. The Yugoslav military had vacated the island and Croatia, a fledgling democracy, was encouraging tourism on Vis.

Starting with the internet phone book from Dalmatia County, we searched the name <u>Repanich,</u> which showed nothing. When we put in <u>Repan</u> it showed 28 Repanić names in Dalmatia County, several on the island Vis. The "ch" was adopted in the USA to replace the Croatian "ć" which sounds like "ch".

We first tried the direct approach and called each of them on the telephone hoping to find a relation. When John asked if they spoke English, they immediately answered, "*Ne ne*" and hung up. *Maybe we should try a different approach.*

John called the hotel on Vis and asked if the proprietor knew anyone named Repanich. Well, yes he did. Their bus driver was an Ante Repanić. When Ante listened to our description of the families in the pictures, he decided he was not a relative. He contacted Jerina Repanić, who faxed us a typed sheet with the correct Repanić family names, relationships, birthdays, telephone numbers and which family members spoke English. The names and families matched the photos.

Our first call was to Dinko in Komiža. His voice exuded excitement to be speaking with an American cousin. He encouraged us to come to Vis, but he said, "three days is not enough". We answered, "We have three free days on the end of our trip and if everything works out, we will come back." *Obviously, we had no concept of the distances or times involved in travel.* We had some concern for our safety as the war was still going on in nearby Bosnia. When we asked him if it was safe to come to Vis, he laughed and told us, "No problem. It is like you are in California and the war is in Montana. Sometimes we hear the NATO planes flying over from Italy, but everything is safe here." With our fears somewhat allayed we made our reservations. John's sister warned us, "They are all communists. They don't even have modern appliances." We had to see Vis for ourselves.

Calls to travel agents to help us make arrangements always prompted the same question, "Where is Croatia?" and the follow-up, "Why do you want to go there? Is it safe?" We abandoned the idea that any local travel agent could help and booked everything through the internet.

Leaving our two hundred acres of walnut orchards in the middle of summer when there was irrigation, spraying to fend off bugs and weeds, and all kinds of possibilities for disaster was a difficult decision for us, but who could pass up free tickets? Carlos, our valued foreman for the past 18 years, assured us he could handle everything and off we went.

Part of our planning had been to check with the Croatian bus service to be sure we could catch a night bus from Zagreb to Split. A representative had assured us, "Busses run all night long about every half hour and you don't need reservations." We had arranged for Sandra, a friend of a relative, to meet us at the airport and get us to the bus station. She and her fiancé, Bruno, were there just as planned and they drove us the slow scenic route to the station telling us about all the sights. They also had checked the bus schedule and had the same information. When we arrived, Bruno went quickly into the station to buy our tickets. But wait...the last bus of the night was leaving in two minutes and it was full. We are not sure how it happened, but somehow when we got into the station two people got off the bus and we got the last two seats in the back of the top level of the double-decker bus.

Our plan to sleep on the seven hour bus trip was quickly scrapped when we saw a small TV with a bright screen playing a terrible, violent foreign movie with the volume turned up so we couldn't shut out any of it. When the movie finished we were relieved and figured we could now get a little shut-eye. The only problem was that no one turned off the TV and it continued its bright light. Now instead of a loud, obnoxious movie we had loud, obnoxious static that went on the rest of the trip. The bumpy, winding road between Zagreb and Split was not exactly the autobahn. Our high seats in the back of the bus magnified every twist and turn. We finally arrived in Split at 7:30 am.

Lounging for two and a half hours on the top deck of the morning ferry to Vis was very relaxing, and although the jet lag urge to sleep was strong we overcame it and visited with folks on board, shared a watermelon with an Israeli family, and saw our first dolphins. We strained to see the first sight of this small island thirty miles from the mainland and kept our eyes peeled until we docked. We had read the following flowery, typically translated English internet description of the Island Rich in Time:

"In the Central Dalmatian archipelago, Vis is the southernmost inhabited land where you can spend your holidays. You can see it already from the Split strait, from aboard a ferry or a catamaran daily connecting Split and Vis. You will discern it standing drowsy behind Hvar and Pakeleni otoci, sharing their fishing and communal destiny through the centuries. It would appear to you in the mist, separate from the sea, only as a silhouette of an island on the horizon, with 585 m high hill called Hum, its highest elevation, a guard-house of all rulers of the island and the sea."

*In the Adriatic geological adventure, it rose above the sea (or it is all that is left from it) as the tenth biggest island among one thousand islands, islets and rocks scattered along the Croatian Adriatic coast, making the bluest sea in the world richer and more desirable for everyone searching his or her piece of paradise on Vis, behind its **blue-eyed waves**- whether only as chance tourist or its permanent inhabitant throughout its history formed by Illyrians, Hellenes, Romans, Croats, each in their own time.*

Changing its masters and rulers, armies and pirates, the island always endured, resisting to all attacks and pernicious influences, in particular since Croats had inhabited it (since 7th and 8th c. A.D.)"

We had read the history and we knew that Vis, because of its strategic position in the sea, had been a Yugoslavian military base for 50 years. While the rest of the Adriatic coast was being developed for tourist trade, Vis was off limits for foreigners. A young man who came back to the island to help it live again describes the island, "Closed within itself, Vis lost breath, grew old, fell behind. Life on the island had visibly melted away as the population decreased."

We had seen the pictures of the stone faced houses, even old mansions, of all sizes and descriptions with their various colors and shapes of red tiled roofs, outlining the protected, horseshoe shaped harbor filled with sailboats and yachts. It was more beautiful than we had imagined and it did indeed seem to have **"blue-eyed waves"**.

CHAPTER 2
DOBRO DOŠLI

We expected Dinko to meet us at the ferry, but we had not prepared ourselves for the warm, enthusiastic greeting from the Repanić family as they met us at the ferry, calling *"Dobro došli "* (welcome). We had not exchanged pictures before our arrival, but somehow they knew us and we knew them immediately. Their excitement at having an American cousin come back was overwhelming. We had a huge sense of relief for having arrived at our destination.

Dinko, a very friendly, balding, athletic man, is the purchasing agent for the hotel in Komiža. Everything he does is with an extra skipping, running step as if he is in training at all times. He learned English in waiter school when he was a young man. From the ferry dock he leads us across the street and under the canopy of palm trees in the park, to his sister Rina's ground level apartment in a plain, unkempt, grey cement building that is sandwiched between two small food markets. I don't really remember how we entered the apartment at that moment, but from then on, we always entered through the open window that faces the street, as the entry door is clear around the other side of the building and it is much too far to walk around. The window is just high enough to get one leg in and then get stuck on the sill before I can get the other leg inside.

Rina carries her large frame in a slow deliberate manner. Her naturally thick, dark hair does as it pleases. Dental work has not been a high priority here. Her attire appears to be whatever was on top of the pile in the morning. Her many years of smoking have no doubt intensified her low pitched guttural voice. She has a few words of English that she has practiced to say to us. It is obvious from the beginning that she loves her island with a passion and wants to share every part of it with us. The island culture is her life and she is not anxious to change any part of it. What was not obvious at first are her remarkable literary talents and wonderful sense of humor. We like her at once.

While Rina serves us a tasty and welcome meal, Drago, her robust, smiling, very personable and extroverted husband enters with their sixteen-year-old son, Stipe. Little did we know at the time how much connection we would have with Drago. Dinko has temporarily disappeared, but Nada, a young woman who also is related somehow, is here to translate for us.

After lunch, we climb into the back seat of Dinko's very small, very old Yugo to drive to the town of Komiža, on the west side of the island. Remember this is the end of July; a 90 degree Fahrenheit summer day. We are hot and sweaty, and fatigue is becoming hard to deny. We roll down the windows of the car to get some air. Dinko warns us, "Don't roll the windows down. The air moving past will make problems for your liver", (or was it kidneys?) We explain, "It is better to take a chance on liver (or kidney) problems sometime in the future, than to die of suffocation in your back seat. What will you do with two dead American cousins?" We compromise by leaving the windows open part of the time. The view driving down the switchbacks into Komiža is gorgeous.

Dinko takes us to his small coffee bar on the Riva, a paved pedestrian walk where the town meets the seaside. He introduces us to his attractive wife, Sonja who greets us enthusiastically in Croatian, assuming we understand her. In the summer the Riva is crowded with tourists and locals strolling along the water's edge, and talking with friends and neighbors. Their coffee bar has mostly outdoor tables in a perfect location under a huge shade tree. Inside there are six more seats. Sonja runs the whole show during the day. She prepares drinks and coffee, washes dishes, waits tables, cleans and enjoys the friendship of neighbors who stop by for their coffee. She works from 7 am until 2 pm, and then walks up the hill to their apartment to prepare a meal for her family. She returns to open the coffee bar at 6 pm. At 9 pm, Dinko takes over for the night shift, and it becomes a sports bar with the small TV entertaining the men of the town. During tourist season, this can go until 2 or 3 am. He works at the hotel from 7 am until 2 pm when he comes home for dinner. He then goes to his fields and garden in the afternoon (or fishing) before taking his turn at the coffee bar.

From the Riva, less than a half block from the coffee bar, Dinko leads us through a narrow opening between buildings and up steep stone stairs to his daughter Maja's apartment. Ah, a king size bed, but we can't sleep yet. We throw open the windows to catch a breeze, but Maja warns us that we may have liver problems if we leave them open. *They are serious about this moving air thing.*

Maja is a follower of the Hare Krishna religion. A young woman named Gunga is staying to help her learn how to meditate. Luck would have it that Maja speaks good English. Her eight-year-old daughter, Sandra, lives part time with Maja and most of the time with Dinko and Sonja, who think she needs a more normal environment.

We leave our bags on the bed in the hot apartment, meet Dinko, and then climb back into the stifling backseat of his Yugo and head out to the family farm. The narrow road from Komiža to the family farm in Dračevo Polje winds up a serpentine and around the edge of the west side of the island with spectacular views down to the sea. The 16th century, picturesque St. Nicholas monastery overlooks the town like a guardian angel. The foot high triangular shaped stones placed on the outside corners about every ten feet as "guard rails" give a false sense of security. On our way up, Dinko explains that the family name is "Sardenjez" which distinguishes this family from other Repanić families on the island. Is it because of their history of barrel making for the sardine factories or did the family originate in Sardinia? No one seems to know.

Dinko translates the name of this valley in the interior of the island. In the Croatian language,"*dračevo*" translates to sticker or weed, and "*polje*" to field. So, John's family farming roots were in a "sticker field". *It figures.* We wind through the valley, past vineyards, and acres of uncultivated land. The little Yugo makes a right turn up a steep, one lane rock road. *Yes, these are solid rocks.* As we pass a large stone house on the way up, Dinko explains that this is not the Sardenjez family farm. Grape vines and assorted fruit trees grow between the rock walls. A line of beehives stands in one corner of a field. The extent of the rock walls and piles began to sink in. They are everywhere on this island. Dinko's little Yugo seems to know how to climb this steep, rocky hill. A little further up the hill, we come to a small stone house with a stone roof. Dinko explains that this was where John's Grandfather Ivan and Uncle Anton were born and raised. The tiny stone house that is now the wine cellar was also the home of Dinko's father, Stjepan and his uncle, Ante. Dinko, his younger sister Rina and older brother, Joško were born and raised in this house, built by Petar, a brother of their grandfathers. Joško and his wife, Vedrana live in this house in the summer and tend their vineyard. The valley below is rich, fairly deep soil with beautiful vineyards, but the steep, rocky hillside land on both sides is productive only where the rocks

7

have been moved away to open the soil. Dinko tells us that in earlier times the Austrian king had the good bottomland and that the peasants had a small plot of hillside land.

THE STONE HOUSE AT DRAČEVO POLJE

Mother Mare has informally divided the land between her children, Rina, Dinko and Joško. (Each of them confided separately that the division was unfair to them). With only the rainwater, Dinko and Joško raise olives, wine and whatever vegetables can survive with no water. They have planted everything between the terraced rock walls, which have been piled over the years to make a space to plant. Their "tractors" are old rototillers.

Dinko leaves us with Joško and Vedrana to go back to Komiža for his evening at the coffee bar. Joško, a wiry, slender gentleman, kisses my hand, instead of the usual "kiss the air on both sides" greeting. In his work life, he was a "non-destructive/ultra sound" weld inspector in the shipyard in Split before he "went on pension". Vedrana was an x-ray technician in the hospital. They have an apartment in Split, which they share with their only son, Siniša, his wife Elza, and two young sons, Pino and Marino. Siniša has the same job in the shipyard that his father had. It is the custom here, that when a couple is married, they movc in with the husband's family. With good reason, Joško and Vedrana prefer to live on Vis during the spring, summer and fall and only go to Split in the winter.

Joško is very proud that he and John are the same age. Even if they don't speak English, they understand many words and with body language that could win an Oscar, we carry on a conversation. We assume that we understand what they are telling us, but in retrospect, we probably filled in many blanks with our own ideas.

From the vine-covered patio, we enter the small stone house through the kitchen where there is room for one person to cook in front of a small propane burner. A narrow stairway going up one wall serves as shelves for jars of homemade aperitifs. On the other side is a bedroom and in the back a small room with an old low couch/bed which doubles as seating for the small table. In one corner is a tiny, old refrigerator. A small television sits in another corner. Vedrana is intently watching a very weepy South American soap opera with Croatian subtitles. Water for the house comes in buckets from the circular funnel shaped cistern, with its slate-like, overlapping stones. We feel as if we are 100 years back in time, but the television brings us back to the present.

Homemade aperitifs with wonderful aromas and strong alcoholic flavors open the meal with salutes of "*živali*", "cheers", "to Sardenjez". The flavors include rose, fig, carob, and anise. My favorite is *orahovica*, a dark, slightly kahlua flavored aperitif made from, of all things, young green walnuts in the hull. The walnuts, with a coffee bean or two and a vanilla bean, sit in the sun in distilled grappa or "*rakija*" for forty days. These forty days are the same in every recipe, so it must be critical. At the end of the forty days, some sugar is added to taste. *In twenty years of growing walnuts, we had never even imagined making anything from the vile tasting, nasty green hulls that we spent many hours and dollars trying to dispose of.* Vedrana explains the wonderful health benefits of this particular aperitif. It will cure anything.

The island specialty, salted sardines swimming in olive oil, was offered as the appetizer course, along with Dalmatian prsut and creamy goat cheese from their neighbor, Darko. Rich, strong red and white wines, newly siphoned from the wine cellar barrels, accompany the first of many delicious meals we were to enjoy here.

Around nine in the evening, Joško drives us in his tiny, old orange Zastava to a concert of the 150-year-old Vis Brass Band in the Kut town square. Kut is the quaint community on the south side of the Vis harbor, which thankfully escaped the drab development of the Yugoslav military and has maintained its historic personality. Stipe, the son of Rina and Drago, plays the French horn in the band. It is a lively, oompah concert with plenty of enthusiastic marches, and songs that apparently are familiar to everyone but us. The children are dancing and the older folks are singing along with rich voices and wonderful harmony. We sit at a coffee bar with Joško and his friends. After the concert, we stroll slowly along the Riva back to Rina's house with Rina talking and laughing and Nada translating. Drago returns us to Komiža to Maja's where we fall exhausted into bed at midnight. What a great introduction!!!! I am overwhelmed.

RINA

CHAPTER 3
SARDENJEZ DAY AT DRAČEVO POLJE

The plan for our second day on Vis is a get together with the whole Sardenjez family at Dračevo Polje. Dinko and Joško organized this "reunion" together. On the way out Dinko confides that he has not been speaking to Joško or his mother, Mare, for several years, because of controversy over the division of the land. They are getting together only because of our visit. This could be interesting. Dinko's training in restaurant management has made him a stickler for details. Everything must be just right and in the proper order. Accompanying us in his Yugo is a large box of whole, fresh sardines, a great excuse to roll down the windows.

Dinko shows us how to sort the sardines. The small ones are cleaned and beheaded for "brodette" or stew and the larger ones are left whole for the grill. I peel and clean about 2 lbs of fresh, young garlic. *Whew, the eyes.* We prepare tomatoes, cucumbers, and beautiful yellow peppers for the salad.

The long makeshift table for thirty people is set just outside the door to the house under the grapevine shade with large bunches of purple grapes hanging down, just waiting to be plucked.

A family of descendants from Petar, the younger Sardenjez brother of Josip and Ivan's, that we were unaware of before our visit, is a pleasant surprise.

Jerina brings an island specialty, pogača, a warm, double crusted thin bread dough with onions, tomatoes and (guess what)...salted sardines inside. Wonderful!! The pogača, aperitifs and the salted sardines open the meal.

Dinko and Joško together prepare the grill with a huge pile of dry grape prunings set into a ground level stone box, open on the front. When they touch it with a match, it immediately flares up into a three-foot high blaze. It burns down quickly to exactly the right coals. Dinko rubbed salt on the sardines, added some native rosemary branches to the coals, then placed the wire grill with the sardines directly over the coals and cooked them to perfection with no smoke or flame.

The wonderful white and red wines (which they call *crno vino*

11

or black wine) flow from Joško's homemade stock, direct from the barrels in the original Sardenjez house. Light deep-fried cookies dipped in powdered sugar, a huge watermelon, and then some Prošek, a sweet dessert wine top off the meal.

After the meal, the women warm a pan of cistern water on the gas burner and wash all the dishes outside in various stages. The children play with a kite and cards, and the adults start singing the Dalmatian folk songs. Everyone puts aside their differences and blend their rich sweet voices into warm, happy, sad wonderful music. I could listen all day. What a shame that most families in America don't have this wonderful tradition of singing together.

THE SARDENJEZ FAMILY AT DRAČEVO POLJE

Off to one side of the house is a newly built small white out building with a toilet and sink. The water for flushing or washing is in a bucket from the cistern. The family proclaims that this is "The John," as John's part of Dračevo Polje. The family had spruced it up especially for our visit. It is the only visible structure not made entirely of stones.

When most of the family had gone, Joško leads us on a walk up the wild, brushy hill to see the rest of the family farm, which at one time the family had planted to lavender between the rock walls. We pick wild oregano, smell the wonderful pungent wild rosemary and are introduced to some of the many other wild herbs on this island. Joško casually mentions that some of the piles of rocks were part of a road placed by the Greeks before Christ.

12

Later that afternoon my first swim in the crystal clear, warm, turquoise blue water of the salty Adriatic Sea has me hooked. To be able to see the bottom, no matter how far out I swim is incredible. Bobbing like a cork transforms me into a gravity free being. Growing up on Bainbridge Island in Puget Sound, I loved playing in the freezing cold water across Eagle Harbor from the Creosote Plant (now a super fund site) every day in the summer. I never knew it was that cold or polluted when I was a kid. This is heaven by comparison. We will return.

Our departure to Russia the next day solidifies our resolve to return for the extra few days at the end or our trip. Almost the whole family that we had met is at the ferry to send us off, singing and waving until we are out of sight.

SINIŠA, MAJA, RINA, MARE. LILJANA, JERINA AND
PERINA GREETING US AT THE FERRY DOCK

CHAPTER 4

OUR RETURN

In the few days on our return to Vis, we are welcomed into each of the family homes. We meet more members of the family including Dinko's daughter Danijela and her newborn son, Jerko. Dinko bemoans the fact that the baby's father, is older than Dinko and that he still has another wife.

Dinko grills fish on the community grill outside the plain, uninspiring communist style, government owned city hall, auditorium and apartment building, where they live in one of the apartments on the second floor. Obviously, he is a master chef and knows just how to cook this fish to perfection. He explains that while he was the manager of the government owned hotel, he had to be "red", so he joined the communist party in order to live in this apartment. Party affiliation was a necessity to keep his job.

Komiža's all night fish festival is in full swing on Saturday night. Several groups of men huddle around various grill arrangements offering free grilled sardines on a thick slab of bread. The pungent odor of fishy smoke hangs in the air. With the benches already occupied by the senior citizens, there is no place to sit down, so it is quite a challenge to eat this traditional island delicacy. We learn to balance it in one hand, remove the unwanted heads, tails, and bones with the other hand without smearing it all over your hands, or dumping it on the ground. *The trick is to leave enough of the bread to use as a napkin to wipe off your fingers and face.* Barrels of free wine tempt us to wash down the sardines and bread. Street vendors selling everything from ice cream to Dalmatian dog helium balloons wander up and down the Riva. A mix of music coming from all corners fills the air making this a multi-sensory experience. We head to Maja's apartment around midnight. Dinko works until 7 am in the coffee bar.

The next morning, we are sitting in the shady courtyard of Jerina and Perina's three hundred year old stone house on a back street in the town of Vis, under a century old grape vine arbor. *Her little concrete and marble table with brick legs would be worth plenty at*

15

an American antique store. In the corner of the courtyard is a bucket attached to a rope, to pull water out of a cistern. Just above the courtyard behind a rotting wooden gate is Jerina's tidy garden with a few fruit trees, the remains of an abandoned chicken house, and some vegetables. The doors, which have long since lost their latches, are closed with a long board propped against them.

The house is a montage of three hundred year old stones, and some red brick blocks that look as if she has started some sort of renovation. At the street level the wooden doors are open to reveal the barrel making shop of her father, Ante. Hand made tools hang on the stone walls, sharp as razors. Jerina demonstrates how her father sat on the "horse" to shape the barrel staves. I expect Ante to walk in and start work, but he has been gone for twenty five years.

As Jerina pours out various flavored brandies, her mother, Perina, and Mare, the mother of Josko, Dinko and Rina, pour out their stories of life on Vis as they remember it.

John asks the question, "Which part of your life was the happiest?" These two old women look at each other, think for quite some time and then agree. "There has never been a happy, easy time. We have always had to work like animals to survive. There was never much time to enjoy the family. We were always working in the field, walking to sell our goods, cooking or cleaning. Now things are not so difficult, but we are too old to enjoy them."   They bring out little crocheted doilies for us to take back to Aunt Winnie.

Petar's branch of the Sardenjez family invites us to their small apartment for dinner. Dario shows us the grossly ugly sea eel that he had caught earlier. He will grill this for our dinner. As horrible as it looked before it was cooked, its taste is delectable. Dobrila, the widow of Petar's son, Antonio, and her two daughters, Liljana and Maja, whom we had met at the Sardenjez family reunion introduce us to the rest of their family. Liljana is a pediatric nurse in the hospital in Split. Her son, Dario lives in Vis with his wife, Ivana and two young sons. Dario is a marine cook on a freighter and spends most of his time at sea. Maja's husband is a former Yugoslavian soldier. She is a kindergarten teacher in Serbia. Their two daughters, Livija and Diana, are students at the University in Belgrade. Maja and her daughters come to Vis every summer for a month's vacation. Her Serbian husband doesn't feel comfortable coming to Croatia. There are many

16

English speakers in this family. We enjoy looking at their family photographs as they proudly show us the pictures of Ante and Dobrila with Tito after World War II. Dario proudly shows us the last boat built by his grandfather. He spends hours with this wooden boat, preserving, maintaining and fishing in it when he is home.

The next day we host, but Dinko organizes, a fish lunch for about thirty family members at the Konoba Bako restaurant in Komiža. We had walked on this street several times on our strolls to swim at the hotel beach, but had never even noticed the restaurant, as it is down some stairs and in the basement of one of the hundreds of old stone buildings. Old amphora and relics from the sea give the feeling of being in the midst of an ancient shipwreck. The waiter brings us fish soup, octopus salad, and scampi that are like small lobsters, smothered in olive oil and garlic, impossible to eat with good manners, but delicious and well worth the effort. Then he brings an enormous grilled fish, head and all, and sets it in front of me. *So what do I do with this?* Luckily, Dinko steps in and skillfully fillets and distributes it. Delicious. As we sit at the tables, we watch the family thoroughly enjoy all the food, sucking the juices out of the fish heads and showing us that the eyes of the fish are "the best part". John has to prove to them that he is "Sardenjez" and follows suit. Luckily, they don't expect me to do the same.

Having emptied several bottles of the best Vis Vugava and Plavac wine, and a few strong aperitifs the family starts singing "Visu Moj", the Vis island anthem. The singing goes on for another two hours. Dinko and Joško both sing bass with Klapa groups (men's a Capella singers). Several of the younger women have won awards in various singing contests. They sing with great gusto and feeling and with four and five-part harmony. Rina has more "gusto" than anyone, but somehow she traded the singing genes for dramatic and creative ones. Her deep, slightly off key voice adds a touch of reality to an otherwise professional quality sound. Instead, she reads some of her original poetry. We can't understand the words, but the response and the attentiveness of the group let us know that she is talented in this arena. As we listened to their laughter and singing it seems as if this must be a regular event. They told us later they hadn't been together as a family for many years, and thanked us for bringing them together again.

We leave Vis the next day, waving goodbye to the family who

has come to say "*Sretan Put*", as we pull out of the Vis harbor on the ferry. We are asking ourselves, "Why were they here and John's family in America? How had their lives differed and how were they the same?" We want to piece the stories together. Our resolve is to come back again and rent a place for the summer. Vis has us both hooked. *Maybe we have found our "piece of paradise on Vis, behind its "blue-eyed waves" as the internet advertising had predicted.*

JOHN, PERINA, MARE AND ME

CHAPTER 5

BACK TO OUR REALITY

John and I returned to the farm and the harsh reality of walnut harvest. **Neither of us could forget our time on Vis.** We jumped at the opportunity to sell our 200 acres of walnut orchards and the house we had built near the Sacramento River in California after farming in one place or another for all forty years of our married life. The Nature Conservancy in its "save the world from farmers" philosophy had offered us more money for our riparian and walnut land and buildings than we could turn down. This deal of a lifetime came to us at just the right time. A crop failure due to frost was imminent. The price of walnuts was at an all time low. The cost of production was at an all time high. Regulations coming down from the state and federal governments squelched the freedom of enterprise that we had enjoyed in the past. Walnut production from China promised to glut the market. Our kids had college degrees, new families and were on to more lucrative, secure occupations. It was time for us to move on.

In December 1999, with the farm sold, we had thirty days to move everything off the farm and out of our house to a house with five acres about thirty miles away in Chico. Carlos and our other farm employees had gone on to new jobs with the sale of the farm. We sent an invitation to the Vis family to choose two men to come to the USA to help us move everything from the farm. The family decided to send Siniša, the son of Joško, and Altiero, the son of Jozo, whom we have not met. We paid their round trip tickets and gave them $1000. They were the best help we could have had. Their stay with us provided lots of opportunities to talk about life in Croatia. A quick, difficult moving process in the rain of winter and over a most unusual, hurried Christmas season and the millennium New Years celebration tainted their perspective of America.

Reestablishing ourselves in another house, deciding that it was not possible to find another farm that would satisfy us, selling and or storing or disposing of forty years of accumulated farm equipment and "what I call junk and John calls treasures" consumed most of our time. We were not ready to sit in a rocking chair and collect our Social Security just yet, but were like the young people who are "trying to find themselves". We pretty much knew who we were, just not what to do.

SINIŠA AND ALTIERO HELPING US MOVE FROM OUR FARM

In March 2000, we had the opportunity to go to the Ukraine for an NGO to present seminars on family farm management to farmers on the Crimean Peninsula. Living with and talking to these farmers for three weeks gave us an extra insight and interest into the problems that people face coming out of communism and into a democracy. The old folks, who had been nominally cared for under the communist regime, were very angry that their promised pensions were gone and many of them were desperately selling anything from old buttons or zippers to a few old clothes on the street. The young people were enthusiastic to try democracy and free enterprise, but with high interest rates to borrow capital to get started, their road to success was going to be difficult. The few jobs that were available paid very little. We could see so clearly that within America's free enterprise system, the ability to own, buy and sell land is a major difference between these farmers and us.

One tractor driver who had been paid by the amount of fuel he used in a day had learned to do some work each day, and then dump the rest of the diesel fuel onto the ground to increase his daily pay. Ironically, he had just received the part of the collective farm that was the same place that he had dumped the fuel, and now that part was not productive.

A welder for the collective farm was holding onto his job without pay, for the security of getting a loaf of bread each day from the farm bakery. No amount of argument that if he were to go on his own, welding for the farmers who were now trying to start their own farms and needed equipment built and repaired, could convince him to take a chance and give up his daily loaf of bread. The problems and thought processes of these farmers sounded like the same seemingly insurmountable problems that the Croatians had told us about.

I made a discovery about myself that was to change our lives. I like to travel, not so much to see many cathedrals, museums and places, as to meet and understand the people, experience their culture, and their family life. I know I will not be happy on tours that speed between cities to view cathedrals and eat in tourist restaurants. I want to know what makes towns, villages, governments and people the way they are. I want to know how the history of a place has affected the lives of the present day residents.

As long as we were in Europe, we thought we might as well tack on an extra week to go back to Vis to find a place to rent for a month or so in the summer. Joško arranged for us to rent an apartment with another John (Ivo) Repanić and a car from Andro Slavić, the owner of AS Restaurant. When we went to get the car, he told us that the owner had taken the car to Split and it wasn't available now. However, Andro told us when he wasn't using his car we could use his. Okay, that will work.

Somehow, we never even looked at rental houses, but became acquainted with a local realtor/attorney, Eta Martinis, a young mother, who spoke good English, and seemed to know the local real estate market. Dinko showed us some property that he knew was for sale in Komiža, and then we headed out with Eta to see what else was available. Serbians who would not come back into Croatia since the war between Serbia and Croatia owned most of the homes for sale.

One of the mostly Serbian communities was on the hillside above Rukavac, a beautiful natural harbor on the south side of the island. All the houses here shared the same problem that we have seen everywhere in the former Yugoslavia. It is never obvious whether they are in the process of building or tearing down. The concrete and block construction starts on the lowest floor (of course). Rebar sticks up on each corner awaiting the time when the owner pulls together enough money to build the next floor, which will also have rebar sticking up

21

for the next floor. Consequently, it is never clear how many floors will be built. If the house between you and the view is not finished, will your view still be there when your neighbor decides to build another floor? Even if the roof is on and tiled, they may decide to take off the roof and add an extra floor. Eta pointed out that it was only a five minute walk down to the sea. What went through my mind was a twenty minute walk back straight up the hill when it is 90 degrees, which negates all the benefits of a swim in the sea. Requirement number one is that it must be near the sea where I can jump in anytime and exercise or snorkel in the clear, warm, salt water.

She showed us another house in the village of Ženka, right on the sea. It would be perfect except that while we were looking, one neighbor brought his mess of fish to clean right in front of the house. We probably aren't going to change that habit, so this one is out. We added another requirement: privacy.

There were three houses available in Bargujac, (pronounced Bar-goo-yachts) a small community on the southeast side of the island. All three were on the sea. Serbians owned all three. All three were only partially completed. The Croatians had trashed all three after the Serbians left. Old clothes, stinky wine bottles, papers, books, and a lot of stuff we didn't care to investigate, were strewn around. Fixtures and cupboards had been taken. Each of the houses could provide some measure of privacy.

That was all that was available that met our requirements.

Wait! We didn't come here with requirements to buy a place. The prices were unbelievably low according to American standards. We could buy half an acre with a sort of house, with good, private access to the sea, in a climate similar to San Diego, for $75,000. Eta carefully explained to us that most of the property on Vis has unclear titles and may be owned by many descendants of the original owner. Many of these partial owners have moved to America, South America or Australia and may not even know they have an interest in the land. The land cannot be sold without the signatures of all owners.

There is no such thing as "title insurance" or "escrow". It is possible for foreigners (or strangers as we are called) to buy and sell land, but not necessarily to own land. *Now that is a unique concept. There must be something missing in the translation.* All the records for the island of Vis are kept by one woman, Isa, who handwrites all the transactions in her books which are piled high around her small office in the town hall, a four story white building referred to as "the white house". Would a fire or flood wipe out all these records? Is there a "backup"? What happens when Isa retires or dies? Another office in the same building keeps track of who is currently using the land and for what purpose. Yet another office keeps track of the maps, which date back to the Austro-Hungarian days. Now the records are computerized.

Eta suggested that with the passports of John's grandparents he could apply for dual Croatian citizenship and then own the land. Through him, I could do the same. We went back to the United States to think about it.

ORIGINAL BARGUJAC HOUSE IN 2000

CHAPTER 6

YOU WANT US TO SEND CASH WITH YOUR SERBIAN BROTHER TO BELGRADE?

With a few phone calls from Eta, a little money in our bank account, warnings from our accountant to be careful, shaking heads from our kids, a gut feeling that this was the right thing to do that overpowered the fear that we were making a big mistake, we decided to buy the property.

We returned to Vis in May, 2000 to consummate the purchase. Eta had informed us that two of the houses at Bargujac had a narrow strip of land between the sea and the house that was owned by "unknown soldiers." The idea of an unknown soldier coming in and building a three story cement unfinished house between us and the sea didn't really appeal to us, so we eliminated those two and decided the other house at Bargujac was the ideal "villa" for us. It had everything we wanted.

Meeting in her small office in Komiža, Eta explained how the paper work would go. She would draw up contracts that she would have a certified translator translate into English. We would then give her $75,000 cash that her brother, a Serbian real estate agent, would take with the signed contracts to Belgrade to have the owner sign. The owner insisted that he would not sign without the money in his hand. We carefully explained that we were not, under any circumstances, going to send that amount of money to Belgrade with someone we didn't know, and that we were not going into Serbia ourselves, as there was still bombing and shooting going on. This could have been the end of it, except for Maja.

We made a telephone call to Maja, John's "cousin" kindergarten teacher who lives in Serbia. We had liked her very much on our first trip to Vis. Her English is excellent and she seems trustworthy. She lives close enough to Belgrade to make the transaction. She didn't have a bank account, but agreed to open one in her town. She will receive a wire from our bank, take out the cash and take it to the owner in Belgrade.

We took all the copies of the contracts to a *Javni Beljesnik* or notary to sign. This in itself is an experience. We came out with copies in English and Croatian tied together very carefully with special red, white and blue string with a gold sticker seal holding the strings together. I think he spent more time tying the string than checking signatures or documenting them. *I wonder what kind of education is needed for this job.*

Meanwhile, we met with several island "contractors" to get their ideas on remodeling the house. One of them was the original builder. He made sure we knew that the previous owner still owed him about $15,000 and he would expect us to pay that first. *That doesn't sound like a good start.* A few others may have been okay, but we decided that if possible, we should try to keep it in the family. Rina's stoutly built, always smiling husband, Drago, is a builder or specifically a "*zidar*" or wall builder. He has several years of education in the specific field. He has been working in Germany and his family home in northern Croatia for lack of a job on the island. His sparkling blue eyes immediately won our trust. He and John seemed to speak the same "construction language" even though he spoke a combination of Zagorski dialect, German, Croatian and a few English words. Many drawings, measurements, and hand motions later, his standard answer to our ideas was "*nema problema*". We looked at some of the work he had done and found it to be top quality. After a lot of talking with Drago and other family members, we agreed that he would start cleaning and remodeling for us. We had to do a lot of explaining about the "new to him" concept of a bonus if he did the work on time and to our satisfaction. Some of the Vis family was concerned that he didn't have much experience in planning and managing. *Well, the whole thing is a gamble, so why not gamble on him.*

We had with us the original well-preserved, but fragile passports of John's grandfather and grandmother, our birth and marriage certificates, and John's father's birth certificate to give to Eta to start the application process for our Croatian citizenship. She told us we can have both American and Croatian citizenship. She assured us that she would send in the applications to the capital in Zagreb and we would have to wait only a few months for approval. She reports that she has made the application to the government for us to own the property. *Did she mention that Americans can't own property here? We don't remember that the subject ever came up.*

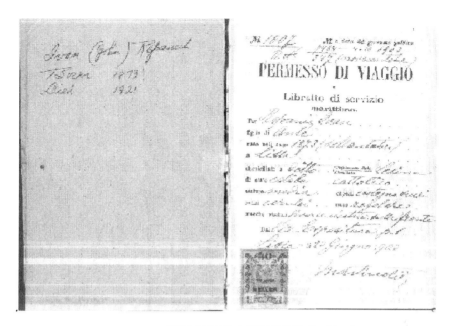

IVAN'S PASSPORT (Italian)

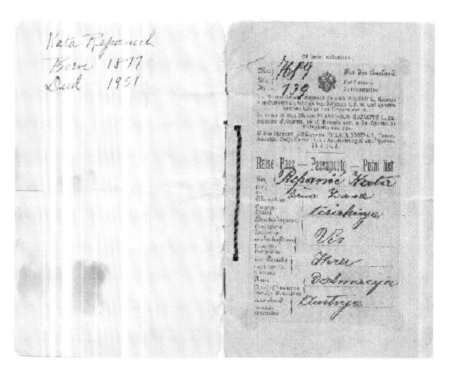

KATA'S PASSPORT (Austrian)

We went back to the US and wired the money to Maja's new bank account. Maja and her husband made the trip to Belgrade in their car, delivered the money and got the contract signed without a hitch. As it turns out, the owner had been a friend of Maja's father and they had a friendly, interesting conversation about old times. She told us later that this had been a very dangerous thing for her to do. If someone from the bank or anyone else knew she had that much money on her person, they could have done her great harm. How do you ever thank someone for taking such a risk?

So now we are the owners *(well not exactly owners until we are "approved" by some government official)* and we have paid cash for a "fixer upper" house, which we choose to call a "villa", next to the crystal clear, turquoise blue sea in the most beautiful location on the Croatian island of Vis. We have put our trust in a distant relative's husband to take our money out of the bank, clean up the house and start demolishing the interior. We don't know the language or the systems here. We have both applied for Croatian citizenship. We justified our decision to ourselves and anyone who questioned us with statements like:

"Life here is like returning to small town America in the 1950's and 1960's which suits us just fine".

"We like everything about this island."

"There is so much to learn here and so many stories to tell."

"It will be a beautiful place for our friends and family to visit."

"This is a great place to use as a base for traveling in Europe."

"Maybe it will be a good investment."

"John will always have a project to keep him busy and challenged."

"Learning a new language in our later years will fend off the Alzheimer's."

"What we save in property tax in buying a place here rather than in California we can pay for our family to come every year."

All that our friends and family could say is "Where is Croatia? Wow, you are brave. We wouldn't even think of doing such a risky thing.

When can we come over?"

We returned to the USA leaving the demolition stage in Drago's hands and an ATM card in his pocket for our bank account. The time had gone by too fast. There was so much more to see and learn and a beautiful Sardenjez family that had so many stories to tell. Why were they here and John's family in America? How had their lives differed and how were they the same? We started to piece the stories together. It took a while, but eventually we put together the following family history.

PART 2
BACK IN TIME

ONE OF MANY OLD STONE HOUSES AT DRAGODID

CHAPTER 7

SARDENJEZ

In the early 1800s, John's great great grandfather, and his wife most likely lived in the remote village of Dragodid, which is loosely translated as "Dear Grandfather". Although we can find no information about them, the family agrees that because of the naming tradition in Croatian families, they most probably were named Josip and Lucija.

The small village of Dragodid is perched on the hill above Komiža, on the Adriatic Sea island of Vis. The people called the country Croatia, a part of the Austrian Hungarian Empire. Over the more recent years, Vis has been part of the Yugoslavian Kingdom, Italian Occupation, English occupation, French occupation, Communist Yugoslavia, and finally the independent country of Croatia.

The Repanić family occupied one of the many small stone houses surrounded by mysterious rock piles and walls placed in the last 5000 years by Illyrians, Greeks, Romans or the Croat people. The extensive rock terraces absorbed the sun and provided a warm microclimate and soil for the grape vines. The porous limestone rocks absorbed the rainwater and held it until the roots sucked it out. Rock walls surrounded the small pasture areas for their goats and sheep. Wine from this island was famous before Christ. Plentiful fish from the sea and a warm, Mediterranean climate made this a tolerable, if not comfortable place to live.

Josip walked along the stone walls and down along the narrow paths cut through the scratchy heather and rosemary, through the shady patches of small pine trees to the fishing village of Komiža. From the tops of the ridges, he stopped to assess the wind direction and the color of the sea. The mild maestral wind coming from the northwest behind him should fill the sails of the Galeta Falkuša for an easy trip to Palagruža, the small island forty-two miles out into the sea. For reasons that only God knows, the sardines or pilchards seemed to be the most plentiful in this traditional fishing grounds for Komiža fishermen. If the wind changed then the journey could take up to fifteen hours of continuous rowing. He and his four friends packed the boat full of barrels filled with salt, drinking water, food and their special and always successful vojgari nets. It was best not to waste time. The dark period between the two full moons was the signal for the boats to race to be first to the island to claim space on the one small beach available to pull up the boats and set up camp. When the barrels were full of sardines packed carefully in the salt for preservation, they started their voyage back to Komiža, before the light of the moon, pushed along by the tailwind called sirocco.

As they came closer to Komiža, the men started singing the familiar song, telling their women to get ready. Their loud, harmonies filled the air between the boat and the shore. The women were ready.

Lucija walked down to meet Josip when she knew the moon and the winds would bring him back. She was always somewhat frightened while Josip was at sea, but it was such a complete happy and warm sense of relief when he returned. She knew the stories of the ones who didn't return and knew how the women had struggled for survival on their own. This time she met him at the dock with the handwritten orders that they must move from Dragodid, to the valley nearer the vineyards, a village called Podhumlje, to work for the Austrian lords in the fields. They would abandon all that they had planted and built together. They must start over, but there may be more possibilities for a good life.

Obeying the orders, Josip "Sardenjez" and Lucija and their small son, Ante, packed their few belongings on the back of their donkey, and into a borrowed donkey cart carrying a barrel of salted sardines and some of their precious vines and an olive tree. Along with their two goats, they walked past the village of Komiža, to the rocky, steep southern hillside of the interior valley to the small village of Podhumlje near Lucija's uncle. They could stay in one corner of his small, crowded house until they could build their own shelter.

They both immediately started to work in the vineyards, pulling out weeds, cutting or tying branches from early morning until around 11 am when the work stopped for a morning meal or marenda. Work started again in the afternoon. They at least came home with some bread and a little wine.

The barrels of salted sardines had not yet run out. Lucija spent some time each day picking edible plants for a delicious salad or collecting the snails that emerged from somewhere onto every green plant after each rain. After hanging them out in cloth bags to clean themselves for few days, the snails made a nutritious soup. The goats were happy to eat the green brush on the hillside and provided some milk and cheese.

On the occasional excursion down the steep hill to the sea, Josip threw his line into the water, knowing that he would bring back enough fish to last for a few days. Lucija collected the small cone shaped shells, and buds from the plentiful caper plants along the seaside, to take home for their sustenance. A bath in the warm, salty sea was so refreshing and welcome on those hot days. Vis was not a bad place to live.

****

Their son, Ante (John's great grandfather) followed a similar pattern of life with his wife, Domina. At some point, they moved to Dračevo Polje.

Domina gave birth in the small house to their first son Josip in 1870. Three years later Ivan was born. The family slowly grew to six children. In the few hours they had for themselves, Ante collected and cut the stones, and slowly built a small stone house and a nearby cone shaped, rock lined cistern to collect the precious rainwater.

They all lived in the little stone house with the roof of thin slate like stone. The ground floor was for sleeping and making wine. Up the steep, narrow stairs was a very small kitchen with a low ceiling that made it impossible to stand erect.

Josip and Ivan played and worked among the rock piles, some of which were graves of earlier inhabitants. They helped move rocks into terraces or just placed them in piles or walls to make room for cultivating grapes or vegetables. Water was dipped with a bucket from the funnel shaped cistern made from overlapping flat stones. They were honed by hitting just right on the side of a larger stone and splitting off a thin slice.

Sunday morning they walked the few kilometers to attend mass in the nearby small stone Catholic Church in the village of Podspilije. The afternoon was the time for social gatherings, singing, dancing and tasting wines and flavored brandies from each household. While the men grilled the sardines, the women prepared the pogača, bread, and salads from the gardens. The women cleaned up, then spent what was left of the afternoon talking together. Bocce games and sharing news that may have come from the men who had left the island to go to far off places occupied the men. The young people flirted and courted their future mates.

Now young men, Ivan and Josip listened carefully to the stories coming from America and planned together how they may someday make their way to this faraway land of opportunity. In America, an uncle, Giovi Žitko, was living in Sacramento and had offered to sponsor Ivan and Josip, as well as some of the other Vis men. He had mentioned in his letter to his brother, Antonio, that he would find jobs for them with other Slav families in California. Ivan, hearing this news immediately wrote about his desire to come to America in a letter to Uncle Giovi.

JOHN AND FRIEND VIEW THE BIRTHPLACE OF JOHN'S
GRANDFATHER, IVAN

Dračevo Polje, Island Vis,

Austria, September 20, 1901

Dear Uncle Giovi,

I am writing to you with the hope that this letter will find you and the rest of your family in good health. I hear from some of my neighbors that you are living in Sacramento, California and are making a good living there. It seems like such a distant place, but we hear there are many opportunities for a good life in America.

Life here on our beautiful island of Vis has changed a great deal since you left here a few years ago. My father, Ante and our family live on the hillside overlooking the vineyards in Dračevo Polje. All the men and women must either work in the King's vineyard or go on the fishing boats for days to catch the sardines. We are only paid with a little food, so we must try to provide for our families from the poor land on the rocky hillsides and with fish from the sea. We have a few sheep and goats for milk and cheese and occasionally some good meat. I have served my time in the Austrian military and I managed to keep enough money to make my passage to America.

I am courting and will marry soon, Katica Lipanović. For now, we will move into my father's very small house with my brothers and sisters until the time that I can find the passage to America. She will stay here with my father until I can arrange for her passage. I have learned the cooper's trade from my uncles and can make fine barrels quickly.

Vis is still the most beautiful place to live that I can imagine, and it will be so difficult to leave my family, but it is more and more impossible to sustain a good life. It seems the best for me and my future family to make our way to America. Can you tell me if there could be a place for me in California? Many of the Vis boys are going to San Pedro for fishing, which is also a possibility for me, but I prefer to continue my farming and barrel making.

I will look forward to your reply. You can post it to Dračevo Polje where I can be found. Greetings to you and your family.

Ivan Repanić, Sardenjez

Dračevo Polje, Vis,   Austria

IVAN CAME TO AMERICA ON THE SHIP
LA CHAMPAGNE

CHAPTER 8

IVAN GOES TO AMERICA

Ivan and Katica were married before the grape harvest and lived at Dračevo Polje with all the Sardenjez. Seven months after he had sent the letter to Giovi, Ivan received a reply from Andre Slavich from Fresno. Ivan immediately started to plan his departure.

Ivan opened his letter to read:

Slavich Barrel Shop, Blackstone Ave.

Fresno. California, USA

June 14, 1902

My Friend Ivan,

Giovi Žitko has written me telling me of your desire to come to California to make barrels, and to be a farmer. He told me that he will sponsor you but you should come here to Fresno.

It is always a pleasure to hear from old friends in Vis. I am sorry to hear of the difficulties you must endure to live there now. I could see this pattern starting before I came to America. How I miss the sea and the island. It is hard to find fresh fish here, and I long for a good mess of sardines on the grill. Fresno is far from the sea and very dry and hot. The farmland here is excellent and has good potential for growing vineyards and fruit. The soil is very sandy and there are NO ROCKS to move. All it needs is water from the rivers to make it the best in the world. The fig tree in my yard is giving me enough for my family and a few to dry and sell. I make some barrels in my small shop and have purchased a little land to someday build a house and farm.

My friend, when you can find your way by ship and train to Fresno I can surely find you a place to sleep in my home and I can use some help in the barrel shop and building on my land. I hope to see you soon.

Greetings to your family and all of Vis from America,

Your friend, Andre Slavich

Ivan would have to find a way to get to either Italy or France, where the ships to America embarked. His cousin, Anton Marinković was planning to leave Vis at the same time and they decided to go together. Uncle Giovi was also his sponsor.

Josip was still in the Austrian/Hungarian army and could not get his passport until he was discharged. It was also the responsibility and the right of the eldest son to care for the family and take over whatever land the family had. The second son, Ivan, would have to go elsewhere to provide for his family.

Dračevo Polje, Vis,

November 14, 1902

Dear Andre,

Today your letter arrived and I felt so happy to know that when I come to America I will have a place to stay and that I can be of help to you.

Katica and I were married in the church in Podspelia a few weeks ago before the harvest of grapes. Most of the neighbors came to wish us their blessings. We cooked a young goat under the bell. Everyone brought food --- pogača, salted sardines, and freshly caught fish for the grill. It was quite festive.

Now we are living with my family in Dračevo Polje. My mother and father, younger brothers Petar and Antonio and my sisters, Lucija and Jerica fill our small house. My older brother Josip is serving in the Austrian/Hungarian army and cannot leave until they discharge him. When he returns, the land here will be his and he will be responsible for our family. It is difficult to provide food for so many. Katica and I must find our own home and do what we can to help our families. Her family, Lipanović of the Miričovi Lipanovićes, is not doing any better, as we all are like slaves to the government, get paid only a little and have only a little time to tend our own gardens or animals.

I am preparing to leave Vis soon to find passage on a ship coming to America. I have obtained a passport. I plan to come with my cousin, Anton Marinković. Many of the other men here are also preparing to leave as we can all see that our only hope for a decent life is to leave our beautiful island. If we could just live here in peace without being like slaves, we could have a wonderful life. I will wait for a ship to America, and then I will find a train to go to Fresno. I will send for Katica as soon as I can pay for her passage.

My hope is to see you sometime soon.

Your friend, Ivan

In the spring of 1903, Ivan and his friend, Anton, set off on their journey to find a way to travel to America. Leaving Vis, they traveled by a private fishing boat to Split, then on a steamship to Bari in Italy. They stayed and worked around the wharfs of Bari, waiting to get passage through the Mediterranean Sea, through the Straits of Gibraltar and up the coast to LeHavre, France. They finally arrived in LeHavre in June and found some odd jobs to pay for their room and board and add to their meager savings. On July 15, the steamship, La Champagne left the port of LeHavre with Ivan and Anton aboard in steerage class with many other immigrants and a little money in their pockets. There was no turning back.

Now pregnant, Katica had kissed Ivan goodbye at Dračevo Polje. She had no idea how long it would take him to make the journey or what hardships he may endure or when she would see him again. The loneliness and wondering filled her heart and mind. The letter she had been waiting for finally arrived.

New York, USA

August 16, 1903

My Darling Katica,

I am in New York in America, arriving on August 9. I cannot believe that I am here. The voyage on the ship, La Champagne from LeHavre, France was crowded with all sorts of people, all looking for a better life in America. We had some bad weather and I was rather seasick for a few days. All I could think of was being with you and living on our beautiful island. During those times, I wondered if I had made a terrible mistake. But now, here I am. This is a very large, noisy city and I have seen some automobiles and other things that I have never heard of before. I can hardly wait to share this country with you.

On the ship, we came past the huge Statue of Liberty standing in the New York harbor with her torch held high to welcome us to America. It was the most welcome sight. The passengers all came up onto the deck and cheered and cried. We have been for the last few days in Ellis Island where we must have health examinations and be registered. There are so many people speaking so many different languages. Now our last name will be REPANICH as they have different letters than in our Croatian alphabet and the ć will be changed to ch. Now I must wait for the train that will take me across America to Fresno in California where I will find Andre. Some Croatians here will help me to find my way.

Please give my greetings to all my family and your family as well. I think of them all every day and wonder if they are healthy and if everything is good for them.

I am so certain that I will find my way and that you and our child will be joining me soon. Being together is what I am working for. You can send your letters to Andre Slavich, Slavich Barrel Shop, Blackstone Avenue, Fresno, California, USA, because, with God's help, I will be there soon to receive them.

Love from Your Husband in America,

IVAN REPANICH

41

Dračevo Polje, Vis

October 15, 1903

My dearest husband Ivan,

You can't imagine my happiness and relief to receive your letter and the good news that you are finally in America.

Now to tell you our good news. Our son was born in our house with the help of your mother on October 9. I had no trouble and am getting back to feeling normal again. Domina will care for him when I must be in the fields. I am calling him Ante after your father. If you agree, I will have his name recorded in the church and have him baptized as Ante Repanić. I have been so anxious to share this good news with you. Our son is a beautiful, healthy boy and is a constant reminder of you and your courage in finding us all a better life. I pray every day that we will be together again soon.

Things are about the same here on Vis. We work in the vineyards most of the day, then walk back to our house to work some more in the garden and tend our goats. Josip has returned from the Military and has planted some lavender and rosemary on the hillside above the house. It is very difficult work, as there are so many stones to move to find a little soil for planting. Thank God, the ancient people moved so many of the rocks before us.

Josip is spending more time with Jera Karuza of Marina Zemlja and I think it won't be too long before they are married.

I look forward to your letters as they brighten my day. I am anxiously waiting to hear from you and be with you.

Your loving wife, Katica

Fresno, California, USA

December 10, 1903

My Darling Katica,

Your letter arrived today and I can't tell you how happy I am to have a son. We will name him after my father, Ante and Anton Marinkovich who has been such a good friend on my journey. His name should be Anton, and the Repanić name will carry on. I pray that you and our Anton are healthy.

The train trip across this huge land took about two weeks with some stops along the way. Some days we would only see a few people in small towns, then vast amounts of land with nothing but brush and sand. We went through some very large cities like St. Louis in Missouri. When we went across the Mississippi River, it seemed so wide. I see many black people that must have come from Africa. There were a few other people on the train that have come from Europe to live in America, and only one other man who speaks Croatian language. I have a paper that was given to me at the train station in New York that tells my destination, so that I won't get on the wrong train. I can see that it will be important for me to learn the American language.

I am now in Fresno and am staying with Andre and his wife. He has many barrels on order and I am working every day to keep up. He has plans to build a bigger house near his barrel shop. I have met some other Slav families living nearby and we will see each other on Sunday at church. I see so many opportunities here, and I am most anxious to share them with you and our son, Anton.

You would not believe how flat this place is. There are no hills, no sea, and NO ROCKS. It is so different from our beautiful island of Vis. The soil is like sand and will grow anything if it has water. In some places, men have made canals to bring the water from the rivers to irrigate their crops. I have seen grapes and peaches, figs, and every imaginable kind of fruit.

America is even better than I had imagined. Please give my love and greetings to all the family and tell Josip that he must start thinking about joining me here.

Your loving husband, Ivan

43

Dracevo Polje, Vis

March 3, 1904

Dear Ivan,

    Our son, Anton is growing so fast. He is a happy baby and is not much trouble. He has learned to smile and make little sounds. He can sit up alone now. To keep him happy, we put some honey on a cloth and let him suck on it. I think he looks like you.

    Josip and Jera were married in Podspelia in February and are now expecting a baby. They are living with us in this tiny house. Ante and Domina are getting older and cannot do as much. Your younger brothers Petar and Antonio are always into some mischief, but they are good helpers. They are attending school in Podselia. Seventeen-year-old Lucija is a good help to Domina, and always wants to be with her friends. Your sister, Jerica and her husband Jakov Marinković now have six children and I think they will still have more. It is good that they are not living here, as we would certainly not have room for such a big family.

    I think Josip is getting a passport and will try soon to come to America. You are always in my thoughts and I hope everything is good for you.

    Your loving family, Katica and Anton

Ivan's brother Josip finally was discharged from military service and made arrangements to join Ivan in California. With great hope for the future, he sent a letter to Ivan.

Dracevo Polje, Vis

March 30, 1905

Dear Brother Ivan,

I now have my passport and enough money saved to come to America. I will be leaving soon and hope to find you in Fresno. Uncle Giovi will be my sponsor and he wants me to come to Sacramento first.

Jera and I were blessed with a son in October, 1904 and we named him Ante after our father. It will be hard to leave them here while I come to America, but we must find the best life for our children. My hope is to bring them to America as soon as I find a job and have enough for their passage. With God's help, I will see you soon.

Your brother, Josip

IVAN AND JOSIP LOGGING IN CALIFORNIA

CHAPTER 9

THE TREE FALLS

Fresno, California

July, 1906

My Dear Family,

Josip arrived in California in April. He was staying here with me in Fresno. He was a big help to Andre building his house on the farm. I was so happy to see him and to hear about everyone in the family. We joined a logging crew to go to the forest to cut down some huge sequoia trees. I had never heard of such large trees, some were more than three meters in diameter. We used very long saws to cut through these huge trees with one man on each end, pushing and pulling. It is very hard work. When they fall, it is like the loudest thunder you have ever heard. We were paid very well and had our room and meals in a large bunkhouse. All was going very well, when one branch fell and knocked Josip down. He had great pain and it knocked the air from his lungs and broke some ribs. He went to the hospital and was there for more than three weeks recovering. Now he is almost recovered, but the American government says he must return to Vis because he is still unable to work and would not be able to support himself. I will stay in America and Josip's destiny will be to return to Vis just because he was standing in the wrong place when a branch fell down on him. Pity.

The Americans will find him a way to get back to New York and then a ship home to Vis. I think by the time he gets back to Vis he will be okay and will be able to work there. I wish I did not have to tell you this news, as I am sure that you all have had your hopes that our families will all come to America. I think of you all every day, and when I see other little boys, I imagine how our son, Anton is growing.

I will miss Josip and am sending the money I can spare with him for you to use as you need. I keep very busy, and I miss you all very much.

Greetings to all from

Ivan

When Josip arrived back on Vis, he wrote to Ivan:

Dračevo Polje, December 1, 1906

Dear Brother Ivan,

After a long journey back to New York, then to Italy and finally to Vis, I am home in Dračevo Polje. I was happy to see everyone here was healthy. My chest injuries have healed well, and I can do enough work. It seems so ironic that by the time I got back to Vis, I was in condition that I could have stayed in America, but so be it. I am in a beautiful place, surrounded by family and old friends with no chance for a wealthy life, and you have many opportunities for a wealthy life in a not so beautiful place. Which is better?

Jera and I have another son we named Stjepan. He was born in November, 1906. The boys, your Anton now age 4 and my Ante, age 3, love to play together and can find lots of trouble between the two of them. They love to follow our father and me around while we tend the animals or work in the vineyard. Your Anton is full of questions, which I try my best to answer.

Katica and Jera are the best of friends. I told Katica all about you and what you are doing. She is very eager to come to America to be with you. I used most of the money that I had with me from America on my journey back to Vis. Mother Domina, Katica and Jera went into Vis to buy food, clothes for the children and candy. I'm afraid that the money is now gone, but the children are very happy. I was hoping to buy some more olive trees or a donkey with it, but now I must wait.

Please continue to write to us and tell us about your life. We hope it will be rich and happy.

Your brother, Josip

CHAPTER 10

FINALLY TOGETHER

Ivan tries year after year to accumulate enough money to send to Katica for her passage to America.

Fresno, California

December 20, 1907

Dear Katica,

It seems so long since we have been together. I miss you and all the family. My strongest wish is for you and our Anton to come to America. I am saving some money and will be sending tickets to you when it is enough and I find a reliable way to get it to you.

I am still living at the Slavich house. He is building another house on his land in the country. I am helping him and learning how to build a house for us. I am thinking about buying some land north of Fresno in a town called Clovis. It is not too expensive and I think it would be a very good place for us to live and to have fruit and grapes. It will take some of my savings but we must have a place for you when you come.

I have seen some of the people from Vis when I went to San Pedro with Andre. They are all fishermen and are doing very well. I am glad, though, that I am here in Fresno with the farming.

Please greet all the family for me. Sretan Bozič and Nova Godina to everyone.

Love from your husband, Ivan

Every time Katica received a letter from Ivan, she hoped that it would have information and money for her and Anton to make the trip to America to join Ivan.

Dračevo Polje

April 15, 1908

My Dear Husband,

    It has been such a long time since we were together, yet I feel as if I am with you every day. I imagine you building with Andre and working in the barrel shop. Anton asks Josip about you. Although he has never seen you, you are very important to him. It is good that Josip was in California to see you so he can tell Anton stories about you and America. Father Ante and Mother Domina like to listen to Josip's stories also and of course I listen to every word and wish we were with you.

    Life is the same here. We have very little and must work hard to survive. We have sickness sometimes, but we are normally healthy. I hope we can come to America soon to be with you.

    Your wife and son,

    Katica and Anton

Finally, after nine years of waiting, Katica opened the letter and found the tickets and money.

Fresno, California

February 24, 1911

My Dear Katica,

In this letter you will find tickets for the ship to America, ($40 for you and $40 for Anton), for the train($25 each) and $100 more for you to use as you need. The tickets are from Trieste, Italy to New York and will leave Trieste on August 22, 1911. You must find a ship going from Vis or Split to Trieste before that. When you arrive in New York, you will go to Ellis Island before you can get on a train to come to Fresno. There you will have a physical examination so try to stay healthy. You must also have $25 with you, so keep enough money to pass the exam and to buy some food on the train. The Slavic Traveler's Aid Society will be waiting for you and they will help you to find the train to Fresno. My address now in Fresno is 611 6th Street. You should ask around in Vis to see who else is planning to come to America.

I have bought some very good land north of Fresno, in the area called Clovis. I have started to build a barn with shelter for animals on one side and a place for us to live on the other side. I stay here sometimes working on the barn and planting some trees and vines. I have planted 20 peach trees and several rows of very nice grapes, some for wine and some for drying into raisins. They are growing well and should start to bear fruit next year. Sometimes I work for Slavich or other men to have enough money to build and for you to come.

It has taken longer than we planned for me to get prepared for you to come, but now it is finally possible. I thank God every day that I am progressing with our plans for you to be with me, and ask him to watch over you and Anton.

I will be eager to hear when you are coming. I hope the family is all well and I send them my greetings.

Love from your husband, Ivan

With this letter in her hand, Katica made all the arrangements for their journey to America. When she had all the preparations and her passports, she wrote back to   Ivan.

Dracevo Polje, Vis

June 15, 1911

My Dear Ivan,

    Anton and I have our passports, tickets and enough money for passage to America. I know that Katina Scirkovic and her four year old son, Roko, will be coming on the same ship. She is going to Bellingham to meet her husband.

    Anton has been going to school for the past year and is a good reader and good with mathematics. I worry that he doesn't know English and wonder how it will be for him in school in America. Certainly, by now you can help him learn quickly.

    Your father has been sick and not able to work much. Mother Domina is also becoming slower and it tires her to work in the fields. She wants to do everything, but must leave much of the work to others.

    Your brother Petar (Nade) is now 17 and is very interested in talking politics. Josip and Jera now have two boys, Ante and Stjepan. They are such good friends with Anton. They will surely miss each other. Josip is thinking of building another house near Marine Zemlja on land of Jera's father. He has asked about coming back to America, but it seems that since he had to come back to Vis he cannot easily get permission to come again.

    Now there are nearly 10,000 people living on our island and it seems like too many. Last year the grapes got a disease called phylloxera and it killed many vines. Many people are thinking of leaving Vis and going somewhere else where they can make a better life. Most of our vines also died, but we will try to get some new vines and replant. Many of the government's vines died, so there are not many jobs left. We are managing with our sheep and goats to sell some milk and cheese and have enough to eat. It will be easier for the family with fewer mouths to feed.

    I am very excited and a little frightened to leave Vis, but I know it is the best for all of us.

    Your loving wife, Katica

Katica described her trip and her happy reunion with Ivan in a letter to her family in Vis soon after she arrived in Fresno.

Fresno, California, USA

November 25, 1911

Dear Family,

Anton and I are finally in Fresno in California with Ivan. The ferry trip from Split to Trieste was quite easy. We waited in Trieste for a week or so before we boarded the Martha Washington. Our trip to America was long and uncomfortable. We were given salted fish, a little hard bread, and water for every meal. I don't know how we could pass a physical inspection with such a diet. We went up on the outside deck at every opportunity for fresh sea air. The smell and bad air in our part of the ship was almost more than I could bear. I was seasick part of the time, but Anton was fine. He and some of the other young boys had great fun exploring the ship and a few times even brought us some fancy food from the rich folks table. I worried that he would get into trouble, but he didn't. We arrived in New York on September 4, 1911.

When we had our examinations, they took Anton away from me and into a hospital for quarantine because they said he might have a disease that they call measles. I did not see him for two weeks. He said he didn't feel sick while he was in the hospital and he probably caused the nurses some trouble. He seems to have picked up some English language and practiced saying the words to everyone on the train.

While Anton was in the hospital I stayed in a large room with other women and my friend, Katina because her son, Roko was with Anton. We were given good meals, but with some very strange foods. Some of the families were sent back to their countries because of their sick children. You cannot imagine how afraid I was that we might not get to stay to see Ivan. After two weeks we were allowed to leave Ellis Island. Some very nice Slav ladies helped us find the train to Fresno and to send Ivan a telegram that told when we would arrive. Katina went on another train to Washington, so we were alone.

The train ride took about 2 weeks with some stops along the way. We enjoyed seeing this very large country from the windows of the train. Anton was always looking for cowboys, Indians, or

---

automobiles.

Ivan met us at the train station in Fresno and took us to the Slavich house where we will live until we can move into the barn and house that Ivan has been building.

Anton is going to a nearby school and is in the first grade. Everything is in English and it is hard for him, but he likes school and will soon be ahead of Ivan and me. He has been in a couple fights with other boys because he didn't understand what they were saying.

This country is very far away and different from our beautiful island. I don't know anyone else here and I stay at home most of the time, except when I go with Ivan to our land to build on the barn to prepare to move into it. I am planting a garden in very fine soil and while I am cultivating it I think about all of you.

Anton sends his greetings to his cousins Ante, Stjepan and Uncle Nade. He says he wishes they were here to play with him. He has not found new playmates that he can speak with yet. He mostly follows Ivan around and is a big help for a child.

I will close for now and hope that you will write to tell me all that is happening on Vis. I do miss all the family, especially Jera.

Greetings from America,

Katica, Ivan and Anton

ANTON AND KATICA ON ARRIVAL IN CALIFORNIA

KATICA AND ANTON TRAVELED TO AMERICA ON
THE MARTHA WASHINGTON

CHAPTER 11

LIFE AND DEATH; VIS AND AMERICA

June, 1912

Dračevo Polje, VIS

Dear Ivan, Katica and Anton,

We were so happy to hear that you had a successful journey to America and are now together. We are saddened to tell you that our father, Ante, became ill in May and died last week in our home. Mother Domina, of course, is very upset and cries often.

We had mass for him in Podspelia and he was buried in the cemetery in Podselje. Now he is with God in Heaven and not hurting. We will do everything to take care of Mother Domina, who is also getting old and weak.

The rest of the family is well, but working too hard for what little we can get out of it. Ante and Stjepan can go to the school in Podselje, but it is a long walk, and many days they don't get there in time, or don't want to go. Ante is doing okay and learning to read. I hope little Stjepan will follow his brother's example, but for now he would rather stay at home and "help" Josip.

We have planted some new vines to replace some of the dead ones, and we are planting more lavender and are cutting the wild rosemary to sell. Our two goats are providing us with milk and cheese, which we can sell. The Vugava wine from Vis is becoming very famous, and if we could plant enough vines, we might be able to sell some wine. For now we have just enough for our family. Josip and Petar go fishing a few times a week to provide fish for us to eat.

We saw Katica's sister, Vica and her husband, Vid Barcič at Ante's funeral. She now has three children, Vinko, Domina and a new baby, Ante. We have shared your letters with the Lipanovič family and they send their greetings.

We always look forward to hearing how you are doing in America.

Greetings from your family on Vis

Josip, Jera, Domina, Ante and Stjepan

611 6th Street, Fresno, CA. USA

December, 1912

Dear Vis family,

We were very sad to hear of our father Ante's death. Please take good care of Mother Domina, as we know she must be grieving. We shall wear our black in his memory.

We have some very good news. Katica gave birth to a son on December 2. His name is Nick John Repanich. They are both doing fine and he is a strong baby. I am working all the time to build our house on the ranch. I also work some other jobs for some neighbors to earn money.

Anton likes school and is now speaking English with the other children. He has some new friends here, but is often talking about his cousins, Ante and Stjepan. He is a good help for me taking care of our grapes and fruit trees.

Katica has some new friends in the neighborhood, but with the new baby, she doesn't see them often.

We are very happy here in America and have enough to live. We are not rich, but are excited for the opportunity to move into our house and maybe buy some more land. We all miss Vis and our family and would be so happy for a good sardine dinner. There are some other Slav families nearby that we see on Sunday at mass.

Greetings to all of our families and friends,

Ivan, Katica, Anton and Nick

Dračevo Polje, Island VIS,

February 13, 1916

Dear Family in America,

We are writing to you now to tell you that Mother Domina died last week after a long illness. She has not been so good since Father Ante died four years ago. She was buried in Podselje next to Father. We miss her terribly, but are sure that she is now with Father Ante again and may be happy once again.

We have not written for a few years and we are sorry for that. We talk of you often and wonder if you are now rich and if you have moved into your house. Do you have any more children?

Ivan's sister, Lucija, and her husband Antonio Zitko now have 2 children. Jakov was born in 1914 and Jakobina was born this year. Antonio is leaving soon for the army.

The war has taken many of the young men from Vis to fight in the Army for Austria. Ivan's brothers, Petar and Antonio are fighting somewhere now in the army. We have no choice, but to let our men leave the island. Many die in the war and do not come back, leaving women with small children to make their own way. We don't know what this war is about, except that if Austria loses we may become Germans or Italians. Does it matter? We will always be Croats in our hearts, no matter who is our ruler. No one tells us much. We only know that our men must go and might not come back. What kind of life is this? Our island, although still beautiful, is not a happy place to live. None of us have jobs. The old men, women and children that are left must grow what we can in our small gardens or go fishing. We trade with our neighbors or sell our goods to a few government men who are the only ones with money. Our children must help us in the gardens and most of them don't go to school. Ante is still going to school some days. We wonder what they will have in their future. Many of the vineyards on the island are abandoned with no men to care for them.

Our hearts are very sad to watch this and our backs are aching from the hard work. We hope that you will write us a letter and tell us about your life in America.

Greetings from your family in Vis.

Josip, Jera, Ante and Stjepan

Clovis, California

December 10, 1916

To Our Dear Vis Family,

　　We just received your letter from February. We are so saddened by Mother Domina's death. We hope that life has improved for you and that Petar and Antonio are home and safe. We wish we could help you in some way, but with the war and the mail service, it seems impossible. We hope this war ends soon, so the world will be a better place for you.

　　Anton is now 13. He is still going to school and doing very well. He speaks English at school and with his friends and Croatian at home with us. It is good that he can speak both languages as he reads the newspaper and tells us in Croatian. He likes to play baseball, an American game. He is good at bocce too. He helps Ivan and me on the farm after school. He sends his special greetings to cousins Ante and Stjepan.

　　Nick is four years old and will go to school next year. Anton is teaching him some English so he will be able to get along in school. It is so important for Nick to learn English and be like an American. We have not experienced any bad feelings, but some Germans and Italians have big problems when they speak their languages. We want our sons to be American. I understand some, but don't know enough to speak to others.

　　Now we don't live in the city of Fresno, but have moved to Clovis on our farm. We have moved into one side of the barn. Ivan has made it comfortable for us, but it is small and too close to the animals. We have 2 cows for milk and a few sheep and goats. He is still building on our house. It is very large and will be wonderful to live in.

　　We have enough vines to make enough wine for us and to sell to our neighbors. We also have Muscat grapes for the table and we dry some grapes for raisins. Our peach and fig trees are now bearing well and we dry most of the fruit in the sun. The summer is so hot and dry here that some days I dream of jumping into the Adriatic Sea and just staying cool. The winters are not too cold but we have many foggy days. I feel on those days like the Yugo days on Vis. The humidity makes my head ache and my bones creak.

Please greet my Lipanovic family, as they don't write to us, but we think of them often and wonder if they are all healthy. We are all in good health and hope that you are also. Our wish is that we will all be together again sometime.

Merry Christmas and Happy New Year

Katica, Ivan, Anton and Nick

Dračevo Polje, VIS

February 17, 1918

Greetings to our cousins in America,

We so enjoyed your letter at Christmas. We are happy that you are happy and healthy in America, but we wish that you were closer so we could be together.

Life is about the same here. Not better but not much worse. Petar is home from the war, but Antonio is not and we don't know where he is or if he is alive. Many of our young men have died in the war. Will we be held by Austria or Italy? It seems as if this little island is like a feather in the wind, floating around for some country to grab for its own. Whoever shall be our owner, we hope that they will consider the people and our existence as important as their riches and power. We hear that some of the returning men shall receive some land as their own. We will wait to see if that is true.

We so look forward to your letters. Don't forget us. We will never forget you.

Love from your Vis family,

Josip, Jera, Ante and Stjepan and all

Clovis, California

December 2, 1918

Dear Josip and Jera and all the Sardenjez Family,

We hope that you are all enjoying good health and that times are not too hard. Our big news this year is the birth of a beautiful and healthy daughter whom we named Mary. We are all in good health and are slowly progressing toward moving into our house.

Ivan is still working at the cooperage making barrels so he has little time to work on the house. Anton is now 15 and like a young man. He does most of the farm work, taking care of the vines and trees. He didn't have school in the summer, so took care of everything here. Nick is now 6 and started school this year. He learns fast and is at the top of his class. He helps Anton a little.

Our Karuza cousins from San Pedro have been here also. Some of the boys help us on the farm when they are here. We want to go to see where they live, but it is hard to leave our farm.

Have you heard any more about Antonio? How has the war affected your lives? Here we hear stories about terrible battles and we just hope that you can avoid them. Some of the German people in America have been treated very badly.

Anton says to tell Ante and Stjepan that he still thinks about them and the fun they used to have together. He has many friends here, but Ante and Stjepan are still the best. We are glad he still remembers Vis and his family. Nick and little Mary may never know about life on our beautiful island and our Sardenjez family and we feel sad about that. Nick can now speak English and he and Anton speak in English together. It is best that he be true American and belong in this country. We will always have Vis in our hearts as our home.

Please greet all the family and our friends

Ivan, Kata, Anton, Nick and Mary

Dračevo Polje, VIS,

March 22, 1919

Dear American Family,

    We think of you often and hope that you are all healthy and that you are prosperous. Congratulations on your baby girl. It is good for her to be born in America.

    Your letters make us feel so happy for you and sad at the same time that Josip had to come back to Vis and that we are not together in America.

    Ivan, your brother, Antonio, never returned from the war, and we heard that he was killed in action. He was a very nice boy and we miss him. He had talked so much of coming to America. It is so sad to lose young men in a war that we don't understand. Many of the young men who went to war did not return. We were lucky to have Petar come back unharmed. Now the Italians have moved onto the island with military and administration. We hear they are not here legally. They do not treat residents very kindly, so we try to stay out of their way and mind our business.

    Petar now owns this land at Dračevo Polje for serving in the Army. He will soon be marrying Lucija Vojkovič and the plan is for them to live here. He is more vocal against the Italian fascists and we worry for his life sometimes.

    Josip is now working to build us a home at Marine Zemlje on land of Jera's father. He is preparing the stones and the land when he has some extra time. We will be happy to live there as the soil is good and it is closer to the sea.

    Ante is now 15 and Stjepan is 13 and taller than Ante. They also miss Anton and think they could find more mischief if he were here. They are helping us now on the land and not going to school. They are both good, hardworking boys but we wonder what their future will be. Ante is helping Petar make barrels sometimes.

    Katica, you will always be my best friend and I still miss you terribly. I wish we could just be together to talk about everything. I noticed in your last letter that you called yourself Kata. When did you change your name? Is it an   American name?

I wonder if you have rosemary, koromač or kadula and all our wonderful natural island herbs in Fresno. I can't imagine living without the wonderful smells and herbs. Do you have an automobile? We hear that everyone in America has an automobile. We are still walking or going by donkey cart.

If you see our Karuza cousins again, give them our greetings. So many people from the island are now in America or Australia.

Love from the Sardenjez Vis family,

Josip, Jera, Ante and Stjepan

Clovis, California

December 15, 1919

MERRY CHRISTMAS TO OUR SARDENJEZ VIS FAMILY

We hope you are all in good health and that your life is better now. We think of you often. We were so sad to hear that Antonio died in the war. We would have welcomed him here.

Anton and Ivan are talking about how they can buy some more land close to our farm. They sit at night and make plans about planting tomatoes and trees. There are great opportunities here, but we also must work very hard. Ivan is still working at the cooperage, but not as much as before. We are closer to moving into our house. Ivan must finish some of the walls. Maybe it will be ready sometime next year.

Anton is now 16. He can do everything on the farm. We have a tractor with an engine to till the fields. I believe it was Ivan and Anton's happiest day ever when they brought it here. We don't have an automobile, but our horse and wagon gets us around better than walking. We still have another horse, but she is old and doesn't do much anymore.

Nick is now seven and is good in school and very interested in the tractor. He came home yesterday with a black eye from fighting with other children. Little Mary is a very happy, contented little girl and likes to pretend she is helping me. It is nice to have a little girl.

Jera, I also miss you. I have some other good Slav lady friends that we see on Sunday at mass, but I also would like to just sit and talk with you. We have some herbs planted in the garden, but they get dry in the summer and just don't have the same taste and smell as they did on Vis. We also miss the fish. Sometimes Karuza brings us some fish, but it can never be as fresh as it is right out of the sea. Someday, we hope to come back to Vis and we will have time to talk about everything. I am now called Kata because people thought it was more dignified for a lady my age.

Love from your American Sardenjez family

Ivan, Kata, Anton, Nick and Mary

Dračevo Polje

June 21, 1920

Dear American Family,

This is the hardest letter to write because we have very bad news. Dear Josip died last week from a very sudden illness at 50 years of age. He had just started building the house in Marine Zemlje when he suddenly became ill with pneumonia. He died eight days later. There was nothing that could save him. He asked that we tell you, Ivan, that you had been his closest friend and brother. We carried him in a procession from Dračevo Polje to Podselje, buried him in the cemetery there, and gave him to God's hands.

We will not move to Marine Zemlje, but stay here at Dračevo Polje in the same small house. Petar has started building another larger house on the same land for his family. They have a baby son with the name of Antonio. Our grief is very strong, as we have lost our husband and father. We will, with God's help carry on. Ante and Stjepan are now 16 and 14 and will have to become men to help us survive.

We wish we could be together more than ever now. We will miss him so, but we will get along.

We wish the news could always be good news, but it is not to be.

Love from your family in Vis,

Jera, Ante and Stjepan

Clovis, California

August 20, 1920

Our Dear Jera, Ante and Stjepan,

Your grief can be felt clear across the oceans and across the world. When we received your letter, we all went to mass to pray for his soul and that you have the strength to carry on without Josip. He was a good man and is surely with God in Heaven. We know that the Sardenjez family will be there for you and help you.

Our Nick had a burst appendix and a high fever. We took him to the hospital where they covered him with ice in a bathtub to cool him down. He is now recovered and back in school. Now, we are all in good health and everything is fine for us now. We are starting to move things into our house. Now we are very busy with our crops, so we will close. Please feel our love and support even so far away. Here is a picture of Nick.

Love from Ivan, Kata, Anton, Nick and Mary

February, 1921

Clovis, California

To our Dear Sardenjez family,

It seems like just yesterday that we received the very sad news of Josip's death. We hope you are getting by without too much trouble.

It is with very heavy hearts that we tell you that Ivan died last week from a very sudden illness. He was so happy to be finally moving us into the new house and things were going very well for us all, then he fell ill and died before we were completely moved in.

Now we are grieving for our beloved husband and father, and we can't even imagine life going on without him. Ivan and Anton had so little time together and were making plans for a larger farming business. Now at the young age of 17 Anton will be the man in our family. He will not go on to school as he had planned but will take care of our small farm. I am so sad that Nick, now 9, and little Mary will not remember much of their father.

Ivan was buried in the cemetery near our small church with many of our friends and neighbors attending. They have been wonderful, bringing us food and praying with us.

Dear Jera, now we both find ourselves without our dear husbands and with boys that are not ready to be on their own. How I wish we could be together to help and support each other. Now Vis is further away than ever. I think of you every day and tears come to my eyes.

We are so sorry to have to send this letter with bad news. Please stay in touch with us. We need each other more than ever.

Love from Kata, Anton, Nick and Mary

CHAPTER 12

LIFE GOES ON: The Next Generation Writes

Vis, Yugoslavia

March 30, 1930

Dear Family Repanich,

It has been about ten years since we have communicated with you. We have not forgotten you. We hope that you are in good health. By now you may be rich and have forgotten us.

We are now living under the King of Yugoslavia and life is not much easier. I will give you an idea of a typical day here. We have a few sheep and a garden. Early in the morning, Jera walks from our home in Dračevo Polje to Vis town to sell some sheep's milk, cheese, wool or vegetables to the rich families that live in big houses. It is a long, difficult walk around hills, over rocks, and up and down rocky paths. When she has no more goods to sell, she walks back up the steep hill to tend our sheep and garden. Mother Jera prepares a midday meal, mostly of native greens, potatoes or beans from the garden. We don't eat anything that we can sell. We get a little sleep in the middle of the day. In the evening, I work a little in the vineyards for other men and Stjepan often walks down to Komiža to go fishing. Sometimes he brings some fish with him. We have only a little time for enjoyment or pleasure.

Petar has finished building a larger stone house for his family. He and Lucija now have two sons, Antonio, and Jakov who was born in 1925. Petar makes barrels to supply the sardine packers and the wineries. I help him sometimes and hope to open my own barrel shop someday.

I hope life is good for you. I often think of our childhood days and the good times we had together. I think we would still be best cousins if our father had not been injured and had been able to stay in America.

Mother Jera especially sends her greetings to your mother, Katica. She wishes there was some way to see each other before they die. Please write to us to tell what you are doing.

Your cousin always, Ante

December 15, 1931,

Clovis, CA, USA

My Dear Cousin Ante,

I have had your letter for a more than a few months. Please forgive me for not writing to you sooner. Now that Christmas is coming close, I think of you often and now have the time to sit down and write a good letter. I am trying my best to write in the Slav language. Since I only learned a little in school in Vis and only speak with my mother and some of our neighbors, I think it is not very good. Please tell me if you understand me.

To let you know about my life I must tell you that after my father, Ivan, died, my mother and I tended the vineyards, peaches and figs. When they were young, my brother, Nick and my younger sister, Mary worked along with us picking, weeding, and watering. We dry our peaches and figs in the hot sun. The grapes are dried for raisins or made into wine by Mother Kata.

The economic times here are very bad with many neighbors having to give up their farms. We have managed to keep our farm, but have just enough money to live and cannot buy anything extra. I work odd jobs around town and Nick found a job in a bakery, delivering pies on his bicycle.

On the weekends the local Slav families get together to eat, enjoy the homemade wines, play bocce, dance and, of course, sing the songs of the old country. We occasionally make trips to San Pedro and Santa Catalina Island where there are many friends who have also come from Vis.

In the summer the Karuza cousins from San Pedro come to visit and help on the farm. The tractor is of great interest to the boys, who all want to drive it. I have warned these cousins not to go through the steep drain but to take the long way around and stay on the road. Last summer one cousin, Tomislav, did not heed my warning and took the short cut through the steep drain, tipped the tractor over onto himself and died. This was a sad lesson for all of us.

Nick and Mary attended primary school in Clovis. Now Nick is in the city of Fresno in technical school, studying the machinist trade. He spends many hours at our neighbors, helping them on their small farm and courting the oldest daughter, Ruth. Her father, Harry moved the family of six lively, beautiful sisters to the country to a small farm, to avoid the "sins" of Fresno. Their mother, Emma, plays the piano for dancing school and various other occasions. All the girls like to dance and sing. Nick has become very American and only speaks "Slav" when he is with our family. Mary helps on the farm and in the house.

So, now my mother Kata, Mary and I live on the farm. I have finished 10 years of school, but cannot go further. I have a beautiful girl friend, Winnie Dulcich, whose parents came from Hvar. Although we would like to marry, we cannot as we both have widowed mothers and families to support. It is our dream to come back to our beautiful islands someday.

I have not forgotten you and will help you when I can. Now it is not possible as we have just enough for ourselves. I think of you often and remember our childhood. How wonderful it would be if your family could be here with us.

We wish you all a Happy Christmas and New Year. Please give our greetings to all of our family on Vis, especially Uncle Nada and Stjepan. Mother Kata especially says to greet your Mother, Jera. Let me know if you can understand my letters.

Please write back. Your Cousin, Anton

Dračevo Polje,

Vis, Yugoslavia

February, 1932

Dear Cousin Anton and family

Bravo, Anton. You can still write in our language and we understood your entire letter.

All the family was together after mass on Sunday, and we read your letter to everyone in the family and many of our neighbors. We know your life is also not so easy and we do not ask for help.

Not much has changed here. Life is still difficult and we don't have too much hope for improvement. We do have some more grapes planted and hope that we can have some wine to sell in the future. We thank God that we have such a beautiful place to live, that the weather is not too harsh and that our conditions will be better in the future. We are grateful for the many natural foods available to us just for picking.

I am learning to make barrels from Petar and make some money from this. Stjepan is an excellent fisherman and is selling and bringing home more fish. We have excellent olive oil from our few trees. Mother Jera sells our wool and cheese and milk in Vis town. She walks nearly 10 kilometers almost every day.

Please keep writing and telling us about your life. We are at the age when all of us should be getting married. Stjepan and I are looking for suitable wives. We read that you have a girlfriend from Hvar. It would be wonderful if you marry a woman that is one of us.

Greetings to all our American family,

Your cousin, Ante and family

Clovis, California, USA

November 20, 1934

Dear Repanić Sardenjez Family,

I am again sorry for not writing as soon as I received your letter. After waiting for a few years for our situation to improve, my girl, Winnie and I were married last year. She works as a secretary. Now we have moved into Fresno. I drive a truck with fruits and vegetables from the valley to the National Park of Yosemite. Mother Kata and Mary still live on the farm and we pay a man to do most of the farm work. They have been very busy on our farm, which is now doing okay. We sell dried peaches and figs and grapes for the table. Kata also makes excellent wine for our table.

Nick, my brother, married our neighbor, Ruth Sager, as soon as he finished his machinist apprenticeship. Winnie and I were hoping Nick would help more on the farm, but he doesn't like farm work and wants a future as a machinist. He works in a shop in Fresno. He helps when we have some big job. Ruth was just about finished with nursing school. She is a nice girl. She doesn't speak Slav and has a difficult time talking to Mother. Her father was not happy that they married so young and without telling the family. He would not see them for a year and we don't see them very often either.

If there is some way that we can help you, please let us know. Would it be best to send money in dollars or goods? Please tell us how we can help you. In this letter I am sending $20. Please tell me if it reaches you.

I hope you and Stjepan find some good women and can be as happy as Winnie and I are. I am sending a wedding picture of Winnie and me.

Greetings to all the Sardenjez family on VIS.

Your Cousin, Anton

You can continue to send our mail to Clovis.

WINNIE AND ANTON

Dračevo Polje

Island Vis, Yugoslavia

November 25, 1934

Dear Cousin Anton

We received the letter with $20 for which we were very grateful.

Congratulations on your marriage. We see from the picture that Winnie is very beautiful and taller than you. We are alike in that way, as I am also a little short.

I will marry Perina Karuza from the village of Duboka soon. She is a wonderful woman of age 26 years. We have known each other for many years. I wish I could offer her a better life, but we will work together for that. She has some cousins living in San Pedro. The Karuza family has a good reputation on Vis.

Brother Stjepan is now in the Yugoslavian Navy. He sends a little money home to us, but we miss him and his daily fish. I am making more barrels on my own. Mother Jera tends our sheep and garden and sells some of it to the rich folks in Vis.

You asked how you could help us. We hear that sending money is not a good idea, as it may not get to us. You can try sending some goods and see if we receive them. It is hard for us to buy flour, sugar, and coffee. Clothes and shoes are also a problem for us. Jera tries to keep up with us, making clothes and shoes, but it is difficult for her. We will be very pleased and grateful for whatever you can send .We all enjoy your letters. We try to imagine how our lives would be different if father Josip had stayed in America.

Your cousin, Ante Repanič

STJEPAN IN THE NAVY

Route 2, Box 222

Merced,California, USA

November 14, 1934

Dear Vis Family,

I hope this letter finds you in good health and that your lives are not too difficult. Things are going well for us now.

Winnie and I are now living in Merced. We bought the trucking business and every day I drive my truck to Yosemite. It is a National Park in the mountains. There are many very beautiful waterfalls. Someday I hope to show it to you if you can come to America. Winnie takes care of ordering and the office part of the business.

My brother, Nick and his wife, Ruth had a baby girl that they named Emarlyn. They still live in Fresno and he works at the machine shop. Mother Kata and Mary live on the farm. With Andro, the hired man, they are doing okay.

In the evenings, Winnie and I play the game of bowling. It is similar to bocce, but with a large heavy ball that we throw down a long wooden floor. We try to knock down 10 pins. I am very good at bowling and my team usually wins. We play it indoors in a large building with our friends.

I am glad you received the money in the last letter. We will put in another $20 in this letter.

We like to read your letters, as they remind me of my childhood days on Vis at Dračevo Polje.

Your cousin, Anton

Merced, California, USA

January, 1940

Dear Cousin Ante,

It has been a few years and there have been no letters from your family. I also apologize for not writing more. Winnie and I work hard from daylight to dark. In the evening, we either go bowling or fall asleep after dinner.

We hope that you are all well and that your lives have improved from when you last wrote. For us, life takes interesting turns. I had an accident with my produce truck. My partner was driving the truck on a mountain road, when for some reason he went off the road. We turned over a few times. I was not hurt too badly, but the truck was ruined. That was the end of that business, as I could not buy another truck. I had an opportunity to own a small gas station so I have worked in that business for a few years. Now I am part owner of a bowling alley in Merced. This job is fun for me as I can bowl whenever I want. I get to travel around California entering tournaments. In 1938, I went to the National Tournament in Chicago with a team from Fresno. I bowled the first perfect game in our town of Merced.

My mother, Kata, enjoys good health and is still active working on the farm, although she has help. Sister Mary is engaged to marry an Italian man by the name of Julio Maraccini.

My brother, Nick lived on the island of Hawaii for a few years working in the shipyard in Pearl Harbor in the machine shop. Now, he and his wife, Ruth live in Washington State. He works in a shipyard in Bremerton. They have two children, Emarlyn and a new baby boy, John, which is the American name for Ivan, named after my father. The Repanich name will go on in the USA for at least one more generation. We see them when they come to California for vacations.

That is enough about our family. Our last letter from you was four years ago. How has life changed for you? I hope it is better now.

Please write and let us know you are all living and how your lives are going. We will not forget you. Don't forget us. Please greet your family for us.

Your cousin, Anton and wife, Winnie

Vis, Yugoslavia

March, 1940

Dear Cousins Anton and Winnie and Aunt Kata,

We received your letter yesterday, and I decided I must write to you immediately. I have sent some letters, but maybe they did not get to you. You have a very interesting life. To make a game into work that pays you is a very good idea. If we were together, perhaps we would be the USA bowling champions, as I am very good at bocce, and win some of our tournaments on Vis. I don't know how to make playing bocce into a job here. I don't know about the bowling game.

I am now married to Perina Karuza and have one daughter Jerina who was born in 1937 and a baby son, Josip, named after my father, Josip. We call him, Jozo. We lived with Perina's family at Marine Zemlje for a while and now have moved into Vis town. I have my own barrel shop and am doing okay. The fishermen and winemakers like my barrels and will pay me for them when they have money.

My mother, Jera, lives at Dračevo Polje with my brother, Stjepan. He is married to Mare Marinkovic. Their first son was also named Josip. They call him Joško. He was born close to the same time as our Jozo in 1939. Stjepan is a fisherman and walks down to Komiža just about every day. He and his friends row out to sea and put out nets. Mare and Jera take care of the garden and a few animals and sell their milk and wool to the rich capitalists in Vis who live in big houses.

Our Uncle Petar, who we call Nade, also lives at Dračevo Polje in his larger house with his wife, Lucija and two sons, Ante and Jakov. He is also making barrels. Our lives are difficult, but on Sunday, we do have a good time with the other villagers. After mass, we go to someone's home, put a goat or lamb on the spit over the fire, play a little bocce and sing and dance for a couple of hours. It is our only time to visit with the neighbors.

Your lives in America are very busy and complicated. Here, life is simple, but difficult. We do hope that some day you can come back to Vis to see us.

Your Cousin, Ante

ALLIED WAR PLANES ON THE VIS AIRFIELD

CHAPTER 13

WORLD WAR II ON VIS

During the war years (1941 to 1945), there was no correspondence between the Vis and American Repanich families. The living relatives on Vis have told the stories of those years.

Italy found its way back to the strategically located island in 1941 when Vis was ceded to Italy in an agreement between Pavelic and Mussolini. The fascist occupation was extremely cruel to the Vis residents. As a five year old, Jerina remembers peaking out of the window to see Italian soldiers parading up and down the streets of Vis. The soldiers would call out to the citizens to come out to get some food for their families, then line them up and shoot some of them. The fascists burned and destroyed houses and vineyards with the inhabitants fleeing for their lives. During this time many Italian words found their way into the language of the Vis dialect. Food was very scarce. There were no jobs other than minding your own vineyards and gardens, or fishing.

With the first hand experience of fascism and the knowledge of the cruelties of the Nazis, most islanders turned to the National Liberation Army partisans, and the anti-fascist movement as their best hope for a decent life. Although the label of "communism" was attached to the NLA, the locals had no idea of the meaning of the word. With the NLA partisans, they had a chance for a better life than anything they had previously experienced. Any other choice could result in jail, torture or death for any ridiculous reason such as giving food to someone. They really had no choices.

The Yugoslav National Liberation Army took the men of Vis, including Ante and Stjepan, into the forces to defend the Dalmatian coast and islands from the Nazi Germans who were advancing and occupying very rapidly. The British and American forces had forced the surrender of Italy and established air bases along the western Italian coast. Immediately after the Italian surrender the Germans began a stronger offensive to take Split and the Dalmatian Coast. Many Yugoslavian military units were transferred to the Dalmatian islands along with wounded soldiers, detainees, and German POWs. Vis became overcrowded and the problems of how to feed and deal with so many people caused a delegation of Dalmatian politicians to go to the Allies in Italy to ask for help. They were successful in getting food and meager medical supplies back to the islands.

As the Germans advanced, occupying island after island, the inferior forces of the NLA withdrew on Christmas Day, 1943 to the islands of Hvar and Vis with many casualties. They had a choice of moving all the operations to the mainland or concentrating all the units on one island. At that time there was no promise of Allied support. They decided to move everything to Vis. Soon Vis became the "Adriatic Fortress" of the NLA with the decision to fortify and organize its defenses. The National Liberation Navy was concentrated in Komiža and in the harbor of the neighboring island of Biševo. Hospitals, shipyards, maintenance units and depots were established on the island. Vis was the only Croatian island that was not occupied by the Germans during the war.

In February, 1944, Vis officially became a war-zone garrison for the Allies and the NLA. About 3700 women, children and men on Vis who were not capable of combat were shipped to refugee camps in southern Italy or El-Shatt, Egypt, leaving an island population of 3500 who were assigned to various duties.

Ante and Stjepan were serving in the Army and Navy and not allowed to come home. Stjepan's wife, Mare, usually alone at Dračevo Polje with 5 year old Joško and 2 year old Dinko, refused to be taken to the ships. When she saw the soldiers coming up the long steep road, she threatened to kill them before she would get on the ship. They turned around and left without her. On the next attempt to take her and the boys to El Shatt she sent Joško out to hide. She told the soldiers she couldn't leave without her son and the soldiers left without them, telling her that she could stay.

Perina and her children, 7-year-old Jerina and 5-year-old Jozo, had packed their few belongings and were ready to board the ships headed to Egypt. Jerina and her friends were excited about going on this adventure to far away places. As she and her mother, holding frightened, crying Jozo's hand, walked up the gangplank, Perina fainted. She and the children were taken to Komiža for medical attention and the ship left without them. Perina and the children had to move from their home in Vis town out to the village. Jerina went to first grade "school" on the hillside sitting on rocks with small wooden slabs for a desk.

When some of her friends or their parents didn't return later, she was glad she had not gone on this adventure.

Fortifications and look-outs were placed all over the island including trenches, pillboxes, barbed wire barricades, mine fields, and high voltage wires to stop any advance from the beaches. From the high hills of Vis, the entire Adriatic Sea could be guarded. The Allies, the NLA, the local population and German POWs built an airstrip in the island's largest interior valley replacing 30 hectares of vineyard in May of 1944. In three months, 215 damaged Allied bombers made forced landings on Vis, saving the lives of at least 1936 Allied aviators. By June of 1944, Vis had 13,500 partisan NLA soldiers and around 2000 Allied troops, mostly British and some American.

One day we saw a Croatian TV crew filming a documentary about the B17 that crashed into the sea about a half mile from our house. Two World War II American Air Force veterans that had been in the plane have been here during the filming. They told us the story of why they are visiting Vis.

"We tried to make an emergency landing on the Allied air strip here, but one wheel would not go down so we landed in the sea. The plane sank deep into the sea. Our co-pilot died prior to the plane going down, but his body was never recovered from the wreckage. A young boy in a rowboat rescued the other eleven men in the crew. Recently a diver found the name of one of the veterans in the plane and traced him down in America. The veteran contacted the pilot and we decided to come back to Vis, together. We had not seen each other since the war. The rescuer, now a man, met us at the ferry. We laid a wreath over the wreckage and said a prayer for our comrade whose grave is in the sea. We will not bring the plane up. "

The NLA assigned Perina and Mare to do the laundry. Mare related her story to us. "We scrubbed the shit out of the soldiers' underwear and laundered the uniforms for the allied troops. They had their living quarters, a cantina and hospital in nearby Podhumlje and Duboka. We built a fire and then boiled a big pot of the precious, scarce water from the cistern, adding ash left over from the fire for soap. After thoroughly hand scrubbing and then rinsing the clothes, we laid them out on bushes to dry. We ironed the uniforms and the underwear with irons heated by the coals from the fire. Our reward was a little food or some chocolate for the children. The children

83

loved the chocolate and the powdered eggs. Occasionally we cooked meals for the troops. We were happy to have the Italians gone and were happy to stay on the island and to help the friendly allies. Some of the English soldiers wanted to take little Dinko back to England, but I could not let him go no matter how difficult it was."

One third of the NLA army were women who fought along side the men brandishing tommy-guns and hanging live grenades from their belts. Any sexual activity between men and women was punishable by death.

Before WWII, Petar and his sons, Antonio and Jakov, were in Tito's communist party secretly. This was during the reign of the Yugoslav Kingdom and the period of Anti-Fascism. Antonio fought with the partisans in the National Liberation Army, but became ill and spent time in the hospital in Malta. Jakov lost his life at the age of 18 in the war.

In May of 1944, the failed attempt by the Germans to kill or capture Marshall Tito, the Commander of the NLA, prompted Tito and his staff to move their command to Vis. The Allies supported Tito as the best choice to command the defense of the Balkans. He took up residence and set up his command headquarters in two caves just above Podspelia until the end of August. At times he also lived in the village of Borovik and in the Villa Tramontana in the Vis harbor. During this time Vis was the seat of the highest civil, military and political bodies of the new Yugoslavia.

The Allied forces began to leave the island in July of 1944 after a successful cooperation with the National Liberation Army. Stjepan was released from the Army with critical pneumonia. With the use of leeches to suck out some blood, he survived. His family continued to eke out a living at Dračevo Polje and with fishing. Ante returned to his barrel making business in Vis town.

When the Allies were gone, Tito's communist Yugoslav military continued its occupation of the island. Life did not improve for the Vis residents, especially for those who did not openly cooperate with the communist or partisan government. Refugees returned from Egypt, many leaving dead family members behind.

When the war was over, Petar's son, Antonio, took a job in the communist government in Komiža. His wife, Dobrila gave birth to a daughter, Liljana in 1945. In 1949 they moved into Vis into their present apartment, now occupied by Liljana's son Dario and his family. Antonio went to political school in 1953 at the age of 33. He finished a course equivalent to secondary school and worked as a spy in secret intelligence. He then went to Zagreb and finished another course for social work in 1958, the year when his second daughter, Maja was born. He was an excellent student. When he returned from school he worked in the government in Vis as a social worker until he went on his pension. After retirement he was a volunteer helping veterans.

After the war, the Yugoslavian government continued using Vis as a military base and closed the island to everyone except residents or military personnel. During this time the army added to the network of tunnels with lookouts and gun emplacements for the protection of the Adriatic coast. The island remained closed until 1992 when Croatia won it's independence in the Homeland War and the Yugoslav military departed.

CHAPTER 14

WAR YEARS IN AMERICA

Although the war was difficult for many American families who served in the military, the Repanich family was not adversely affected.

In Merced, California, Anton wanted to join the military to defend his country, but could not because of injuries resulting from his earlier trucking accident. Instead, he joined the civilian fire department for nearby Castle Air Force base. He was able to continue operating the bowling alley. When Mary married a soldier of Italian descent the farm was sold to their hired man, Andro. Kata lived with Mary or with Anton and Winnie for the rest of her life.

Nick was in a vital civilian job at the United States Naval Shipyard in Bremerton, Washington and he was asked to stay there rather than serving in the military. He spent many nights as a civilian warden, protecting their town. Ruth served in the Red Cross. The war was almost transparent to Emarlyn and John, whose lives went on as usual.

JERINA IN HER KITCHEN WITH THE LETTERS FROM
THE USA REPANICH FAMILY

CHAPTER 15

HELP COMES FROM AMERICA

John and I spent hours listening to the stories of these second cousins' difficult childhood years during and after the war. One day Jerina brought out a box containing the letters that John's Uncle Anton and Aunt Winnie had sent to their family in Vis after the war. They were all written in the Croatian language. Another time she brought out a clean, well pressed "Springmaid" sheet and a man's shirt that had come in one of the care packages. These had to be 50 years old.

The letters from Anton and Winnie were translated into English and I have composed the others, assuming what might have been written by the family on Vis from my interviews and discussions. I make the assumption that these letters actually would have made it through mail inspections. I know some of them were actually received by Anton and Winnie, but most likely, the family tells me, many were confiscated.

After the war had settled down and Ante was back on Vis with his family, his curiosity about his cousin in America was always on his mind. One day he sat down to write a letter to find out what was happening in America.

Vis, Yugoslavia, March 17, 1947

Dear Cousin Anton,

It has been many years without writing to you and for that I am very sorry. You must know the war years were very difficult for us. But most of us survived. Our family lost Jakov, Petar's son. Now I hope that this letter will find you and that you are in good health and maybe by now a very rich man. Our families here are mostly struggling to keep going. I have my barrel shop in Vis, which is doing okay, but it is just enough to live with nothing extra. Our daughter, Jerina is 10 and our son Jozo is 8 years of age. They both go to school here in Vis. Mother Jera lives with us in Vis. During the war, I had to serve in the army and lucky for me I came home. My family had very hard times in the wartime, but thanks to America and England the war is finished.

We still have the Yugoslavian army on Vis and outsiders are forbidden to come to the island. The army has made fortifications all around the island for the defense of the Adriatic Sea. Many areas of the island are not accessible to the people here because the army has built tunnels, wire fences and many areas have dangerous explosive mines. Large trucks are always driving on the roads. Soldiers are in every corner of the island and most are from Serbia. They seem to like our women, so we must be careful. The ships of the Yugoslav navy fill up the harbors in Vis and Komiža. Vis is a very different kind of place now than it was when we were young.

I spent six months of hard labor in prison in Split because I mentioned to one of my cousins, a son of Petar's who is strong in the communist government, that one large grape farmer should not have to join the communist cooperative. I just said that he would make more profit independently and therefore pay more taxes to the government. We must be very careful what we say and where we say it.

My brother Stjepan and his wife, Mare, have 2 sons, Joško, age 8 and Dinko, age 5. They will have another baby soon. They still live at Dračevo Polje. Stjepan is a fisherman. Someone coming to Komiža told us that your mother remarried to an Italian. Please tell your Mother Katica to write to Mother Jera and tell her about her life. Jera talks about her friendship with Kata often. We hope that we receive a letter from you with all this information about you.   *Your cousin in Vis,*
Ante

Anton was delighted to hear from his cousin, Ante and took time from his busy schedule to reply.

Merced, Calif.

January 30, 1948

Dear Cousin,

I have received your letter which found us, thanks to God, in good health and I am extremely happy to hear about all of yours and that you are, thanks to God, all in good health. I know that you have suffered a lot and hope that you will be better very soon. As far as I know it will be much better in the future.

I am happy to hear that your mother, Jera, is still alive. What is with Uncle Petar? There is a lot of time that I hear nothing about all of you. I would like very much to know what you are all doing and how things are going.

Now I wish to inform you what is with us here. I am married and my wife, Winnie is one of ours. Her parents are from Stari Grad on the Island of Hvar. We don't have children. My brother Nick is married to an American. They have an 8 year old son, John, and a 14 year old daughter, Emarlyn. They live 400 miles away from us. My sister, Mary, is married to an Italian and they have 2 daughters of 6 and 2 years.

Mother Kata is still alive and is in a rather good condition. She has not married again since our father died. If someone told you that she is married to an Italian, it is not true. Maybe they were thinking of my sister, Mary.

Now I wish to tell you what I do and with what I am occupied. I tried to do various jobs. Now my wife and I have a small coffee bar in the city (Merced) and we bought a farm 4 miles outside the city.

Last year we sowed grain and we have 10 acres of tomatoes so we are now working days and nights. It is not possible to explain to you everything in this letter but step by step I will inform you how things are here.

I am sorry if I don't write correctly but you know very well that I did not finish school in Vis and I think it is a long time since I have been writing in our language. I am doing my best.

Now, my cousin, I will try to help you if you tell me what is most important for you. I am sending you 20 dollars in this letter but as cousin Vojkovic says, you do not need money as much as you need some goods. We will send 5 packages to your address that will be marked as follows.

Ante Repanić; Petar Repanić; Jozo Repanić, Ante's son ; Jerina Repanić, Ante's daughter, Jera Repanić

We are informed here it is better to send in this way than in the one name. If we have forgotten someone, please share with them. I will not send anything in your wife's name. But in the pack for Jera are enough things for your wife and mother so they could divide them.

I do not know Petar's address, so I will send them to your address. I do not know if his wife is alive or not so we did not send anything for her. Write me please who is alive and who is not of our relatives.

Thank you for telling me what you do for work and how you live? We live good, thanks to God; not just us, but everybody. We are not rich but we have enough for our needs. Here everything is very expensive now but we hope it will be less expensive in a short time.

Dear cousin this is all in this letter. Please greet all there. We wish that God will give you all good health and we will do our best to help you. Write me if you receive all the packages and if everything comes in a good condition. Please send me photos of you and your family if you have any. I will send you our photo in the next letter.

Now once again greet all of yours from all of us here

I remain always your Cousin

Anton Repanich

Rt 2, Box 730

Merced, California, USA.

If God gives us to be healthy and if other things go well we will see each other before we die.

Vis, Yugoslavia

April 15, 1948

Dear Cousin Anton,

We received all the packages you sent to us and were very grateful for everything. The dry eggs were especially useful. My wife, Perina has found many ways to use them. Someone in the family can wear all of the clothes. We all thank you so much for thinking of us and helping us. We hope the time will come when we will not need help from outside, but for now it is very good to have these things.

Stjepan and Mare now have a baby girl, named Rina. Now they have two boys and a girl. They all still live at Dracevo Polje in the small house. They have a very hard life.

We have no pictures of our families, but we hear that there is a man in Vis town who can do this for us. We shall try to send some pictures.

Greetings to all of our American family. We do like to hear from you and hope that we shall see each other in the future.

Your cousin, Ante

Merced, California. USA

August 15, 1948

Dear Cousin Ante,

Let me write you a few words after a long time. First of all we are all in good health thanks to God, so I suppose it is the same with you and your wife, children and mother.

Sorry I didn't write you earlier, but many times I would think about writing, but I was working long hours and when I had some time to write it was late in the evening and I went to bed.

I have not forgotten you. Almost every day Winnie and I talk about you. If it is possible for you please write me. I always like to read your letters. Tell your wife I have received her letter and now I am answering her.

And now I am informing you that Nikola Zitko visited us before he traveled back to Vis. I have received a letter that he arrived there in good health. I believe that you have seen him. I gave him some money for you and I believe he gave it to all of you. Since that time Winnie and I have sent 4 packages to your home and 3 packages to Stjepan and one to Uncle Petar.

I hope you receive everything in good condition. Nikola will tell you how it is here and I think that he has arranged in New York to send you some food.

We would be extremely happy if you would have some photos taken to send to us. We would like photos of you and the children and of Aunt Jera. Could you also ask Stjepan's family to send some photos?

Dear Ante, if God gives us health and if our trade goes well, Winnie and I will come to visit you, but I don't know when. Tell Aunt Jera I will come there and bother her as I did when I was a child.

If it is possible for you and your wife and children to come to America, write me and we could obtain what is necessary and I think we could settle for your travel expenses.

Now I will not write longer, but just say hello to your wife and children and Aunt Jera and all of our relatives and friends.

Tell your brother Stjepan I will write to him one day and ask him to see about a package that we have sent to him. Please tell Uncle Nade that a parcel will come to him too.

Now, a hearty hello from me and from my wife and mother and all of us. Mother specially greets Aunt Jera.

I remain your Cousin, Anton Repanich

Meanwhile, packages of clothes, food and special little treats arrived at various unexpected times. The children were getting the idea of a benevolent benefactor in America. The names Uncle Anton and Aunt Vinca (the Croatian name for Winnie) were becoming very familiar. There were always a few squabbles about who would get the jacket or pants.

Vis, Yugoslavia

March 30, 1949

Dear Anton and American Repanich family,

     We are so grateful for the packages that we received. Stjepan and Nade also received their packages and asked that I tell you thank you very much. We think that everything came as you packed it. We can make good use of everything. The children especially enjoyed the small toys, especially the rubber balls. This was something new to them. They only play with rocks and small dolls that they create from scraps of material or seeds.

     Sadly, we must inform you of the death of Uncle Petar (Nade) at the young age of 55 years. He leaves his wife, Lucija and one son Antonio who is married to Dobrila Borčić. They have one daughter, Liljana who is about 4 years old. His other son, Jakov was killed in the war. He was living in the larger house at Dračevo Polje that he built. Now Lucija will live in Vis with Antonio and Dobrila.

     You mentioned that sometime we should come to America. Dear Cousin, nothing would make our family happier than to come see your beautiful country and see you again. For us that is impossible, as we could never save enough money to have passage. If you could help some of us, we would certainly try to come. Maybe it is more possible for you and your wife to come to see us on Vis. Even with the restrictions, we think you could come as family. Let us know if that is possible and we will arrange for you to come back to our beautiful island. You would find it quite different now, as the military has ugly buildings, tunnels, fences and many soldiers.

     I told my brother, Stjepan, to bring his family to Vis town to have a family picture taken. He said that he would make a good effort to do it soon. I shall also see that we get our photo taken to send to you.

     The family is normally healthy, sends their greeting, and thanks to you for your help.

     Your cousin, Ante.

Route 1, Box 780

Merced, CA

October 4, 1949

Dear Cousin Ante,

Here I am sending you a few words. We received your letter, and all of us were so happy to hear from you. We were so sorry to hear that Uncle Petar died, because he wasn't very old, and I'd always thought the day would come that I would at least see one of my uncles alive. But, thank God, what is meant to be must be, and now he has gone on to a better place.

Now, dear Ante, forgive me for not answering your many letters both from you and from your wife, but if you only knew how much work we have to do here everyday maybe you wouldn't be surprised. We sold our coffee bar and now we live in the country. We built a new house but we are not doing so well. Our crops failed this year due to disease and we lost all our tomatoes. Now all we can do is look ahead to next year.

You must be very busy now. When we picked grapes over there in Vis there was lots of wine and we were able to sell what we didn't use for home use. If you were here your daily wages would be $20/day. Here the grapes they use to make wine are very large.

My mother and sister came for a visit just yesterday, and your name came up in the conversation. It would be great if all of us could meet together to sit and visit one day.

Tell us how you are doing, and how is Stjepan? Are you on good terms with each other? Now that there is no longer an older person running the family affairs, everything has fallen on both of your shoulders, so try and help each other as much as you possibly can. Now, dear cousin, I won't go on any further, but instead close this letter with my sincerest greetings from me and my wife and all of us in the house. Let God give you, your wife and children all good luck, happiness and good health.

Remaining your cousin, Anton Repanich

Vis, Yugoslavia

November 15, 1949

My dear cousins in America,

I shared your letter with all of the family. We are surprised that you are having problems with your crops and we are very sorry for you. You tell us that we could earn $20 in a day in America. We are lucky if we see that much in a month here, but we trade this for that...barrels for fish, wine for meat, or work for barrels. We get by that way, but we have no extra money. So you know we are always grateful to receive any help you can give us. We understand that now you also are on hard times and don't expect you to send anything.

The family is well except for Stjepan's oldest son, Joško. He is ill and needs an antibiotic like penicillin to get better. We cannot get it here and now. If you could send some for him, the whole family would be very happy and he would have a good chance to recover.

Now we are picking olives, which we will press into oil. Our grapes were good this year and we have made more wine than before. We don't make enough to sell, but just enough for our family.

Our children, Jerina and Jozo are going to school in Vis. Stjepan's children go to school in Podspelia. They all are smart and good students.

God Bless you and all the Sardenjez in America.

Your cousin,   Ante

August 1, 1950

Rt 2, Box 786, Merced, California

Dear Cousin Perina,

Here I am, writing you a few words for the very first time. These few words are to let you know that we are all in good health and we hope that this letter also finds you in good health as well as all the members of your family.

I hope you will be able to understand my letter because I don't write the best "naski" (Croatian dialect). This is because I never went anywhere to school for it, but I learned it at home when I was a child.

Today we sent one package of soap and one package of food. Give half of the soap to Stjepan and all of the food is for you. I want to send you some clothes, but I will wait for your reply because I would like to know the children's ages, clothes sizes, and shoe sizes they're wearing now. It is hard for us to buy because we don't know what will fit them. So, write me immediately and send me their sizes, and don't forget to send me your shoe size as well as Ante's and Teta Jera's shoe sizes. If it is at all possible, tell me in American sizes or draw around your feet on a piece of paper.

I have no other news to share, other than to send you our dearest greetings from Anton and me, and send you heartfelt greetings to your husband, children and Aunt Jera. Anton will write a letter to Ante soon.

Your friend, Winnie Repanich (Vinka, wife of Anton)

Rt 2, Box 786, Merced, California, USA

November 15, 1950

Dear Cousin Ante,

Here I am finally sending you a letter after a long time. A few words to let you know that, thank God, we are in good health, and hope that you and all the members of your family are also in good health by the time you get this letter.

Today my wife was very happy to receive a letter from your wife Perina containing sizes for everyone, especially the papers with the drawings of your feet. Now we will know just what to buy. Winnie has wanted to send you clothes for some time now, so now that we have the sizes we can send them in the not too distant future!

Some months ago we sent Stjepan some penicillin for little Joško. Already three months have passed and I'm not sure if he received the first package of penicillin. I would like to hear how the little one is recovering.

We were also wondering if Stjepan would like to send Josko here to stay with us here in America, if possible. He has two sons there with him, and it would be better for the boy and for Stjepan. I still haven't received an answer, so I don't know what to say. We sent you and Stjepan some food, and I think that you have probably received it by now since two months have already passed.

On our side, we are now picking cotton. On our farm we also have cows for milk and for beef. My wife Winnie has more than 1000 chickens and sells the eggs. She loves to ride around the ranch on her horse to check the fences. This year we planted 50 acres of cotton and it looks good.

How are things over there? I heard you had a good grape harvest with lots of extra wine. How many barrels of wine did Stjepan produce, and did you end up selling some?

Sincerest greetings from all of us here. Best regards to your mother, wife, and children and all our friends and relatives in the old country.

Your cousin always,

Anton

Soon, the women were corresponding regularly. Jerina prepared lavender sachets and fig cakes to send to her American benefactors. She felt very close to Aunt Winnie. Perina crocheted doilies and made lace to put in the letters.

Vis, Yugoslavia

November 30, 1950

Dear Cousins Anton and Winnie,

I must write to tell you how much we all thank you for the packages. Everything you sent is useful. The children especially enjoyed opening the packages. Times here are hard, and we just barely get by. You were very clever to send us just what we need. I am sending more measurements of other family members.

I am also sending the pictures of our family and Stjepan's family. He brought his family to Vis town on the donkey. It was a big adventure for the children, as some of the little ones had not been to town before. Maybe you can tell from the pictures how big we are. We especially need shoes and you know that walking on the stones is very hard on shoes.

Stjepan and Mare say that when Joško is well and strong, they will think it is a good idea for him to come to America. Thank you so much for thinking of us. Maybe our Jozo could also come to America.

Perina Repanic, Wife of Ante

Now years later, Rina remembered the trip from her home at Dračevo Polje to Vis as a three year old, to pose for her family photographs. Hrvatska Zora, a literary magazine featuring Vis authors, published this story. The translation to English follows:

My First Encounter with Vis Town

By Rina Repanić Gotal

I was born two years after the Second World War and have two brothers before me. Thank God, we all know how hard life was in those days. There were all kinds of problems, and most of all we had sickness, hard work, and hunger. We were always in clothes with patches on top of patches, and the three of us grew up just like wild grass.

Once in awhile, we would smile over an unexpected occurrence of good luck and happiness. A letter with a package had come from my father's cousin, Uncle Anton, in America. Like many Croatian immigrants living in America, he was making miserly wages, but he intended to help us out, as well! He had sent us some clothes, but he didn't know the children's sizes. He would be thrilled to have a picture of us all, so he asked us to please sit for a portrait as soon as possible, so he could send us clothes in our sizes.

Ha... that was easier said than done! Didn't he know that in the sticker fields of Dračevo Polje there was not enough paper to wrap a homemade cigarette, much less to get a family portrait? Did he know he was requesting the impossible of us? We were over our heads with work just to survive. The walk to town was long and treacherous....and with three children, besides!!

My father, Stjepan, could have easily let the matter drop, muffled by his mutterings about the impossibility of it all, but he did not. His only thought was, "if that's what we must do, then that's what we'll do; especially for our dear uncle in America who had already helped us so much." Despite the obstacles involved, he made an appointment for a sitting.

My mother, Mare, always had more work to do than was possible to complete. Now she had to get father's suit out of storage to air out. The suit reeked of mothballs, and the best place to air it out was in the valley before Sardinjizovo and under Serenjoka, the

100

sunny side, where every wind in the world seemed to blow. Brother Joško said he needed new shoes, and brother Dinko's shoes needed mending. They had holes in them from playing too much soccer, despite Mother's warnings!

With all the extra work in preparing for our photo, Mother instructed the boys to lend a hand with the animals. First, they must pick good leafy branches of bushes and good edible greens for the young lambs and goats, and then gather two bags of dry pine needles and dry leaves under the trees to let the animals roll around in, to keep them clean and dry. The animals were penned up so we could prepare our clothes for the photograph. The wooden frame on the saddle needed reinforcing and the ropes were looking frayed and weak.

And so, little by little, task by task, the big day came to go to Vis to have our photos taken. We got out of bed when it was still dark outside. Mother took care of the animals, put the chickens in their pens with a fresh supply of wheat shells and kernels of corn.

Then she called for us to come in and get dressed. Now, things began to get interesting. My ten year old brother Joško protested and complained that he would not wear the too short and too tight jacket from America that didn't suit him. Set aside for eight year old, Dinko was the black jacket which Joško had already worn and outgrown which he loved dearly and called his "black crow". It was dear to me as well, and I could hardly wait for my turn to wear the jacket! But, that was not important. The important thing was that it was now Dinko's jacket and he would wear it for the photo. But Joško had never intended to give him that jacket, his dear "black crow", not for all the tears and punches in the world. Mother got the situation under control with a good thrashing with the leather belt for both of them.

She dressed three year old me in the fancy, American-made rose-colored dress with short puffy sleeves, a white embroidered collar with cross-stitching and pockets in the form of a heart. This dress had been in one of the packages from America, and gave us good reason to let them know our sizes. I was plump and round and the dress was tight on me. Over the dress, I wore a small tight-fitting jacket, which made me look even bigger. I felt as full as a balloon.

101

Only our father didn't complain. His old, dark, pinstriped suit, brought out of storage only for funerals or weddings, didn't show even a bit of wear, nor was it too short or even too tight. The only thing was, when he bent over a little you could see it was a bit snug around the paunch, but not much. Over a white shirt, he tied his only tie, put a hat on his head and went outside. When mother changed from her normal working clothes into her dark dress with the tiny white checkers, brushed her hair and pushed her hair behind her ears, we knew that we had to go.

Ready and waiting outside in the yard was our donkey, Vesna. She listened attentively to us with her big gray ears turning around like speakers, pursed her lips together, blew out, showed us her teeth and made loud donkey sounds while our father began to arrange the three of us children on her back. She seemed to know something was unusual about this day. Dinko sat right behind the animal's head and would sit up front on the saddle. I was in the middle of the saddle in a small wooden chair, and Joško was right behind me, sitting right on the animal's ass. After all, someone had to hold on to me.

That is how we traveled down the side of the Mardesic property. The biggest problem was that Vesna would barely walk, as if her legs were stuck in black tar. When we arrived at the top of Petrova's property, at the very first grapevine, she began to jump and run back toward home. The clever beast had realized that this time we were on a long trip, and she had not counted on going all the way into town! She would have liked to come only as far as the closest grapevine! She was very smart and very clever.

We somehow managed to reach Konteju, where the main road is now, then downhill to the Lokvica water reservoir, then up to Roko's property and under Liznjokovo, an ancient Greek road built on the top of one of the hills in the main field.

I started to make a fuss. I pleaded to stop to visit our Aunt Doma, my mother's sister who lived nearby. I knew she would give me biscotti dipped in the sweet red wine called Prošek. I had already had enough of this donkey ride! The wooden luk of the saddle was digging right into my back, and we were not even close to Vis town!

Never mind how I carried on. No one paid me a bit of attention and on we went. When we reached the crest of the next hilltop we all called out in excitement because from here we caught a great view of the Vela Gospa bell tower in the village, Podselje. We stopped to say a prayer. But not even here would they give me a chance to dismount. The saddle had given me blisters right on my baby fat and my poor little bottom was being poked from the hay coming out from a hole in the saddle. How uncomfortable! But continue on we did, from the crest of the hills, to the plains, and into a deep canyon.

Underneath a carob tree along the way, my mother told us we were now half of the way to town. "My dear Madonna," I thought to myself, "if we keep going like this all the way to town, they will have to bring me in just bones. All my flesh will be rubbed off from all the constant bouncing and bumping. Or else, they won't be able to peel me off the saddle! They definitely won't be able to take my picture. What a shame for our American uncle, especially since mother had said that this was something nice to do; that to send him a family picture would give him something to smile about. "

Then the miracle happened. The Madonna herself heard me and answered my prayer! In Vino Polje, they took me down so I could walk a little. I was so numb and uncoordinated from the ride that my knees buckled up beneath me. My legs had no feeling, in fact. I trembled a little and walked from side to side like a drunkard. Father said, "You are not doing so well and we can't hold your hand." His hands held onto a ten liter jug full of his homemade wine. Mother was carrying a large bag in her hands and balancing on her head was a large basket full of gifts for the many relatives we would visit while we were in town. So, I had no choice but to be lifted again onto old Vesna! The best thing was that Dinko had been so proud to be first man in the saddle. Now I would be sitting up front.

This is how we passed Vino Polje and Borova Njivu, a flat area with the shade of pine trees. We came to the top of Luskega hill. In front of me was the deepest blue I'd ever laid eyes upon. If I looked downhill, one side or another, all I saw was a deep and ominous blue. I felt immediate panic with the hairs on my head immediately standing on end. To my young eyes it resembled a blue, bottomless pit; like an endlessly huge laundry-cooking pot, without any upper edge or handles to hold on to; bigger than any you could ever imagine, full of some strange blue goo inside. I held on with all my might to that small wooden piece of a saddle until it was smashed into my fingers and my heart was beating in my throat. My God, did we come to heaven today? Or is today, of all days, the end of the world when the sky, I was told, is supposed to fall into the earth? Fear gripped me, my body stiffened up, and I was unable to shed a single tear.

Behind my back, my parents encouraged me "Don't worry, that's only the sea." Since when didn't I know what the sea looks like! From Rebrinjoka not far from my house I had seen the sea and I knew all the islands by name. There were the islands of Susac, Korcula, and Lastovo and even Palagruža; sometimes you can see it and sometimes you can't. I'd seen boats of all sizes traveling across the water, including fishing boat expeditions with nets and lights when my father rowed when the men went to sea to catch sardines. Of course, I knew at the edge of the horizon lies that small fine line where the sky meets the sea, and if you follow that line, you can't go wrong. But this was something different, – a huge blue ball shape, bluer than anything I had ever seen before.

And our Vesna, walking with the attitude of "This is definitely not my job," unconcernedly shook and bounced us three children, veering from far left to far right as she took wide steps up the side of rocky-terraced Luskega hill behind the school in Vis. When we got to just below Kapelica chapel, I could hang on no longer. There, I could see my destiny before me. For that deep blue cooking pot contained a huge ugly mouth with ugly, red teeth, missing in places and lying directly in front of me! "Mother of God, look, now I'm a goner. Watch, everyone, I will fly over the donkey's head, right into the deepest depths of the blue lips with those terrible, red teeth." My throat was gagging, and I began to explode in tears, "Help! Pick me up, quick; I'm falling down into the sea. Can't you see? The sea is going to eat me!"

They could see that things were getting serious and so they quickly dismounted me. I began walking again, but because my legs had no feeling, and my emotional state was not so good I didn't even notice the stones beneath my feet. I lost my balance, fell, and scraped my shinbone darned good. I didn't even notice how fast the blood was flowing until it began to bleed through to my stockings. I thought to myself," better to have ruined my stockings than for the sea to eat me with those with those huge, ugly blood-red teeth. "

Then I could see that I was approaching the sea all the same, and I just could not go on any further. I sat down on a rock and

104

couldn't go forward or backward. Father stopped the donkey, took my brothers down, tied the wine jug and mother's basket to the beast, and took me by the hand for the remainder of the trip down into town. As far as I was concerned, not even the sea could upset me now. In my father's hands I felt perfectly safe. In those hands, which had dug with a pick-ax so many acres of earth, moved so many stones to make room for a few vines; which had rowed so many vessels across stormy, battering sea and which had dragged in so many nets filled with hordes of fish. Those small, worked to the bones hands with undernourished arms and withered muscles were for me my great rescuer as we completed our journey into town. As we descended into the town, the large red teeth became the red-tiled roofs of the houses lining the very blue sea along the Riva, and my fear vanished.

We went to a room with shuttered windows where we prepared ourselves a little. We fixed our hair and changed into good shoes for the picture. We took the saddle off Vesna and tied her up under a carob tree, then made our way to Stipe Kaceus, the photographer's studio.

He sat us down on chairs, positioned us and repositioned us for different poses and said to us rather coarsely, "OK, SMILE!" We were bewildered, and besides that, who could smile after all that we had been through? He ducked his head into some box-like container all covered up with a big black cloth and moved a little bit towards us. I was afraid of the camera. I thought we were going to die; and he wanted us to smile? And when all of this was finished, I asked my mother, "A, ma? When will he start taking our picture?"

When all of this happened, I was only three years old. I still have the photo from that day, and I would not give it up for all of the photos in the whole world.

Rina Gotal Repanič

MARE, RINA, JOŠKO, DINKO AND STJEPAN

JOZO, PERINA, JERA, ANTE AND JERINA

Merced, CA

Route 2, Box 780

March 7, 1951

Dear Cousin Perina,

We received your dear letter and it made us so happy to hear that you are all healthy and happy. The pictures of your families were wonderful and we will treasure them always. It is so good to be able to see the faces of each of you when we think of you. Mother Kata especially enjoyed seeing Jera. She says she was surprised to see that Jera looked older, as over the years she had continued to think of her as the young woman she knew on Vis.

I received the measurements you sent. They are all good. We were happy to hear that you received the food and soap and so we are hopeful that the clothes we send will also arrive without any problems. When you receive them, write us to say what you received in each packet. Then we will know what you did and did not receive.

We received a letter from Teta Lucija and she wrote that she received our packet. She said it made her happier than we will ever know. We also hope that Teta Jera will be thrilled with the contents of her packet, as well as all of you!

I won't go on any further. Please receive all our best wishes and greetings.

Your cousins always,

Winnie (Vinka) and Anton

June 12, 1951

Vis, Yugoslavia

Dear American Cousins,

We received your package and were all so happy with all that you sent. Ante and, Stjepan were so happy with the pants and shirts. We all now have new shoes, thanks to you. Jerina especially was happy for the new shoes, as she was making our shoes from the rubber from old wrecked airplane tires and the skins of our animals. Mother Jera was very happy with her new dress and has been wearing it every day. The boys were very happy with the rubber balls and also pants and shirts (but especially the balls and candy).

Thank you so very much. It makes us feel so good that our family in America has not forgotten us.

Your Vis Cousins, every one

Merced, CA

August 9, 1951

Dear Cousin Perina and Cousin Ante,

Just to let you know that we are healthy, and expect that you are the same, enjoying good health! This letter is from both Anton and I, because Anton is overwhelmed with work right now. This year we planted cotton and there's much to be done right now.

We want you to know that we sent a few packages of food, plus clothes for the children. The food will come in Ante's name, and the clothes will arrive in Jera and Jozo's names, as follows:

In one large packet will be 100 lbs of flour. In another packet will be 20 lbs pasta and 10 lbs pasta. In another packet will be: 3lbs canned meat, 10 lbs rice, 5 lbs coffee, 5 lbs pasta, 1 lbs pepper, 5 lbs sugar, 5 cans of milk, 5 lbs shortening.

In another packet will be 5 cans of meat, 2 cans of chocolate, 2 cans of beans, 1 small box of tea and 1 small box of sweets.

In Jerina's packet will be: 10 dresses, 2 pairs of shoes, 6 skirts, 6 nylon stockings, 6 handkerchiefs, 6 blouses, 5 pairs of underwear, and 1 jacket.

In Jozo's packet will be: 1 jacket, 2 dress shirts, and 2 pants. 6 shirts, 1 belt, 1 pair of pajamas, 1 pair of shoes, 4 handkerchiefs, 3 pair of underwear, 3 undershirts, 1 T-shirt, 5 pair of socks.

2

All of these packages will be posted from New York. We prepared the packages here and sent them to a friend in New York. Better to send from there so they can be insured, whereas from here we cannot insure them. You will also receive them much faster than if we sent them from California.

When you receive each packet, immediately write to us everything that you received so we will know that you received all that we sent to you! Don't wait until they all arrive. Instead, write us each time you receive each packet.

We have moved from the country into town.

Our address is now:

355 E. 17th Street

Merced, California

Similar packages have been sent to Stjepan's address.

I must close this letter. Sending our best greetings to you and your children and of course to Teta Jera.

Your cousins always,

Winnie and Anton Repanich

Vis, Yugoslavia

November, 1951

Dearest American Cousins, Anton and Winnie,

Your packages all have arrived and we are so happy to receive them. The packages all came within one week and took one month from New York.

Our situations here are improving. Jerina and Jozo go to school here in town and are doing well. Stjepan's children go to school in Podspelia. We all still struggle, but we think times are getting better. We still have Yugoslavian military on the island. We must all attend the communist government meetings and our children go to the government children's clubs.

Petar's son Antonio and his wife, Dobrila and daughter, Liljana also live in Vis town. Aunt Lucija lives with them. Antonio and Dobrila are very active in the Yugoslavian government. He makes barrels and boats.

We received everything that you listed in your letter. We will certainly have a Happy Christmas with all of these things and we will be the best dressed citizens of Vis. The sizes of the clothes are all very good.

Stjepan and I hope our sons, Joško and Jozo can come to live with you in America. They are both twelve years old. We know it was our father Josip's dream to raise his family in America. They would have a much better life with you than we can provide for them. We understand that they will have to work hard and study hard, but they are ready for it. We think it is best for both boys to come if it is possible. They are both good boys and smart.

Thank you very much for all of the things in the packages. If you could send me a small handsaw and a drill for my barrel shop I would be very happy. I have made all the tools for my shop, but it is most difficult to make a saw. If you know of other tools that would be helpful please send them also

It is very hard to know where to send our letters as it seems that you move from house to house very often.

We very much like to hear from you. I must tell you it is easier for us to read the letters from your dear wife, Winnie, but any letters are good for us. We wish that you have a Happy Christmas.

Your Vis Cousins,

Ante, Perina, Jerina, Jozo, Jera, Stjepan, Mare, Joško, Dinko and Rina

JERINA AND JOZO

Merced, CA   March 15, 1952

Dear Cousin Ante,

    We received your letter a long time ago, and please forgive me
for not writing sooner. First of all, we must say that Winnie and I are
in good health, thank God, except for the fact that we lost our dear
mother, Kata. The poor lady was in pain for a long time, about two
years. On October 14, 1951, she had a small stroke and we
immediately took her to the hospital, where she lived another three
days. And so, dear cousins, we remain saddened and a little
bewildered and I am ashamed to say I didn't write to let you know
about her death. Now, the whole world knows and I still haven't
written anyone.

    When we think of Kata's life we admire her courage. To leave
her family in the old country and come to America with a small boy
was very brave. She was a wonderful, loving mother. She always let
us know how she felt and how we should behave. There was no
question that she expected us to be good and work hard. She was a
tough business woman when it came to running the farm. No one else
compares when it comes to cooking and her wines. They were the
best. Although she understood English she rarely spoke anything but
the Slav language, but she always checked the obituaries in the
newspaper to see if any of her friends had died. She was always the
first to help another family in need.

    It makes me very happy to hear that the quality of life is a
little bit better there than before. I know that it's still hard for you,
and I'm sorry that we can't help you as much as we would like to.

    In the last 3-4 years everything has gone backwards for us.
There seems to be nothing I can do to get and keep a little money.
Last year we planted cotton and everything went wrong. Rain and
damp weather ruined the crop, but only here, nowhere else, so I lost
all the money I had and I must ask the bank for credit for next year's
crop. I will try again next year and see what happens because the
location is good. If everything goes according to plan, I could
accomplish a lot. I haven't sent you your hand saw and those other
little things you requested, but I did not forget you or Stjepan. When
I get a chance, I'll take care of it for you. But believe me; things are a

little hard for me now. This unbelievable crop disaster which happened only here really knocked me flat. I'd like to have Joško and Jozo come live with us, but there is no way that we can do that now. When we see how this year's crop goes, we will be able to think about it seriously again. And now dear cousin, I want to send you this small letter with a picture of Nick's children, Emarlyn and John. Don't wait to write just when you get my letters, but write whenever you can because I really want to hear from you and I will never forget you. When I am able I want to help you in any way I can.

Here are many greetings from me and my wife and many warm regards to your family, and please don't forget my dear Teta Jera. I send my greetings as well to Stjepan, his family, and all of our dear relatives in the old country. Sorry that I don't know how to write very well. My dear wife does very well at everything. Wishing all of you good health.

Your Cousin Always, Anton Repanich

EMARLYN AND JOHN

September 27, 1952

Dear Jerina,

We are so sorry that we didn't receive the letter which should have come around the same time as your package. After we got the package we checked our mail everyday in hopes of seeing your letter. After some time, after still not hearing from you, we wrote to your mother saying we received the gifts from you and everything was in good order and to thank you for us. So all this time we thought your mother received our letter and that we would be hearing back from her, but no! Instead, to our great surprise, she never received our letter! We find it amazing that your mother never received our letter and that your first letter was never received by us. Now, this letter will be sent by registered mail so we'll know if you receive it and you can answer us as soon as possible to reassure us that we are in contact with no missing mail.

We thank you so much for everything because it made us so happy to receive a package from you, and even more happy that you did it on your own initiative. We especially like the Lavender sachets that you made. The picture you sent shows us what a beautiful woman you are. You look somewhat like Anton's sister, Mary. It is like having part of the island and our family right here. This is something we will never forget!

Dear Jerina, when we moved from the country into town we lost your measurements so we would like that you send them again to us as you sent to us once before. Write us and tell us what you need. We will look around and see what we can do and ship the best quality goods we can find. Tell your cousins to write to us and send their measurements as well. For now, I have nothing more to write except to send you our dearest regards and greetings to you and your father, mother, brother and Teta Jera.

Remaining your unforgettable cousins,

Winnie and Anton

Send our love and good wishes to Cousin Stjepan, his wife and children.

116

Merced, California

October 12, 1952

Dear Cousin Ante,

Here I am, after a long absence, sending you a few words to let you know that I haven't forgotten you. We are healthy, thank God, and hope you are the same over there.

A long time ago you asked me to send you a saw and a drill (to make a wooden barrel). Over here, we don't have a barrel-making place and so it's a little hard to find supplies, especially the saw you need. Now I have managed to gather a few things together and so I'm sending them along. If you need something else write me and I'll look for what you need.

I know that I'm a little late, but as I wrote before, for some time I had no time to be in contact, but now we are a little better. Just today we began to harvest cotton and it looks a little better this year. So far, everything is going o.k.

Dear Ante, Now I am in the position to bring the young ones here if you agree that it would be a good thing. Write immediately so we can discuss how this would work out. I will of course do whatever I can to make it happen. But it will not be an easy life for them; that much I can say right now.

It would be very good that the boys come here, because it's a good opportunity for a young person. In America there is plenty of work with good pay, and for children good schools. We would take care of them as if they were our own. Since I have no son of my own, this would be a great pleasure to raise these boys and to have them to help me on my farm. If this is going to happen then someone must start working on this right away.

Write and tell me how you are doing, your family and especially Teta Jera. I would love that you were all here with us, but thank God, this is the way it has to be.

Now I won't go on much further, so write if there is anything else you need and I will look around for you.

Now I send you my best greetings, from the whole family,

Remaining your cousin,   Anton Repanich

Vis, Yugoslavia

December 4, 1952

Dear Cousins Anton and Winnie,

We received your letter yesterday and are ready to help you to bring our boys to America. We have asked our cousin, Antonio who is Peter's son to help us on this end. He says that the boys will need a number from Yugoslavia which is now very difficult to get. Tito is not allowing many people to leave our country. Antonio is close to the government and seems to have some influence. He says he will try.

One of our mother's cousins, Domina Karuza is nearly blind and would be very grateful if you could send her some strong eyeglasses so that she might be able to see better. We told her we would ask you if that is possible.

Mother Jera is living with us and in reasonably good health for 84 years. She has good days and bad days. She was very sad to hear that Kata died and she wonders why she is still living. She often tells us stories of their times together in old times. She says that having the grandsons of Josip's go to America would be the happiest time for her. She says that Josip's greatest dream was for his sons and grandsons to have the best opportunities. If he could not stay in America and his sons could not get to America, then it would be wonderful for the grandsons to go. She is so pleased that you would want them to come. She keeps talking about how the tree fell on Josip and changed everyone's lives.

Our family all sends their heartiest greetings to you for Christmas and for the New Year.

Your Cousin, Ante

La Grande, California

February 14, 1953

Dear Cousin Ante,

After a very long time I am writing you a few words, first of all to say we are both, thank God, in good health. I hope that when my letter arrives it will find you and your family in very good health.

My brother, Nick's wife Ruth passed away suddenly in January. They still live in Washington State, so we don't see them much. His daughter is already in college and his son, John, is 13 years old. We feel very sorry for their loss, and hope that John can come to spend some time with us on the farm. Nick is in politics in his city of Port Orchard and is also a good bowler.

I received your letter a few days back. I was glad to hear from you. I am writing back right away, I guess, because I am already looking forward to hearing again from you. Don't think that I have forgotten you. For me it is the hardest type of work to write a letter. So if too much time passes and you still haven't heard from me, please write me again.

First of all I want to inform you what's going on with young Jozo and Joško. We wrote to the Washington Ambassador but we haven't had a response to our letter. Then we wrote to the Consulate in San Francisco and he wrote us that it is impossible to bring the young ones over here to live without an identification number both from here and another number from Yugoslavia designating them eligible to come to America.

It might in fact take years to get this number permitting them to travel and come alone to Los Angeles. We know a Croatian lawyer and he told me that now it is practically impossible for them to come here as we had planned. The only possibility would be if a person who already has permission to come to America is unable to travel; one of the boys could be allowed to travel in his place.

I have looked into every possibility. I went to San Pedro and visited an agency. They told me they couldn't help me. Then I wrote to a New York agency and they said, without the visa number from Yugoslavia they could not help me. Then I contacted the American Red Cross, and they said they also cannot do anything for me. Now, if you know any other options, let me know and I will be willing to do it. We would be more than happy to bring the boys to the States to live with us, and to do whatever will be necessary to make it happen.

Dear Ante, I am sorry that I haven't helped you this year financially, but believe me, I want to help you again as soon as I am able. For the past 3 or 4 years everything has gone backwards for us, but I believe it won't always be this way.

I sent you and Stjepan each twenty dollars, both of you, bank to bank, so you will be able to receive it in the nearest bank. If you have a bank on Vis, then they will know you. If not you can go to the closest bank and will have to show identification. You can buy food and any other needed items over there.

Tell Domina Karuza that I will look into sending her glasses but for now I can't do it. But I won't forget and when I am able I will take care of it. Write and tell me the best way to send them there.

What is the exchange rate now between Yugoslavian dinars and one American dollar? How many dinars would twenty U.S. dollars bring you?

I won't go on any further, but hope and pray you and your loved ones are happy this holiday season. I wish both you and Stjepan all the best. Don't be lazy like me about writing back!

Accept our sincerest greetings from me and my wife, and many happy regards to everyone over there. Let God give you all good health and much happiness. And I will never forget you.

Remaining your cousin, Anton Repanich

Here is my new address: Rt. 1, Box 89, Le Grand, CA, U.S.A.

Vis, Yugoslavia   *April 4, 1953*

Dear Cousin Anton and Winnie,

We have tried everything on this side to find a way to get the boys to America, but it seems that now it is impossible. Many young men from Vis are secretly escaping on fishing boats or in other ways. Our boys are too young to try that so we must wait and see what we can do. We are sorry that it will not be so at this time, but now we all know that we have tried. We truly thank you for your efforts and wishes. We will keep up our family vineyards so that when our boys are old enough, they will have something. The wine from this island is still famous around the world. We just can't make enough of it to get rich.

I had surgery for a stomach problem. I had to spend one month in the hospital in Split. Now everything is okay. My wife Perina took care of the business selling all the barrels that were finished. Now I must work quickly and long hours to get ahead of my customers.

We are sorry to hear about your bad luck farming. We always think that if you are in America everything is good and okay, but you tell us that even there things can go wrong. We all hope that things go better for you in the future.

Stjepan and I both have tried to find the $20 that you sent to the bank. No one here or in Split seems to know where it is or how we can get it. It is better to send it direct in the mail as we have received it that way before.

Petar's son, Antonio has asked if you can send some guns and ammunition to him. I don't know for what purpose he wants them, but he is strong in Tito's government. I said I would ask, but that it may not be possible to get them. He went to a school for the secret service for the government. We all must be rather careful what we say.

I see from the pictures that you sent that you are starting to get some white hairs. I guess we are all getting older, but it is hard to imagine you as an old man, I still think of you as the 8 year old cousin that left Vis more than 40 years ago.

Please greet your family for us, Your cousin, Ante

January 20, 1955

LeGrande, California

Dear Cousin Ante,

We received your letter some time ago, and more than anything, we are happy to hear that you are all, thank God, healthy and that your operation was a success. Without good health, everything else is no good.

Winnie and I are healthy, thank God. The only thing is that we must work long hours. We have a small café that we work in at night, and during the day we are working at home or in the fields.

Dear Ante, I am deeply ashamed to write. Now I have many years and every letter I must send, I hesitate because I know I write badly. I don't have a hundred words to say, but frankly, everything for me has gone completely haywire.

This year I planted 40 acres of tomatoes and everything looked good until we started harvesting. When we started to sell them, the price of tomatoes dropped to nearly nothing and there is nothing I can do about it. I am now in debt, so I am anxious to make some kind of financial headway. My wife and I decided to take charge of a small café in town to make a few dollars. I must again try to have a good crop next year. But thank God, both of us are for now good and healthy and maybe everything will turn around for the best.

Well, enough of bad news. You wrote that I have started to look older, and it's true. My hair has started to turn white. I remember when me and my brother started farming, I was twenty years old. He is nine years younger than me and his hair is whiter than mine! But besides having white hair now, I am thank God in pretty good condition. My wife has started to get a few white hairs herself, but she looks good and I guess works harder than any other woman here who is years younger.

You wrote that you will give your son your vineyard, which is more important than money, because the day has come that without a vineyard and a good education it will be hard to make a living.

Nick's son, John, spent part of the summer with us helping me on the farm. He is a fine boy who likes to hear stories of my life on Vis. It is good for me to have a young boy to tell the stories to. He is very interested in the farming and the only Sardenjez Repanich in America.

More than anything, I am sorry that we can no longer help you as we did before. But, thank God, maybe the day will come that things will be better.

As for the guns. Please tell Antonio that it will not be possible, nor would I want to send any guns to a communist.

Now, dear cousin, I won't go on any farther but send to you and everyone there our greetings. We hope that you have a much happier New Year and that everything goes hand in hand exactly as you would like it to be.

I wish the same for Stjepan and his family. This we wish for all of you, both me and my wife, from the bottom of our hearts,

Your cousin always,

Anton Repanich

Rt. 1, Box 89

Le Grand, CA

WINNIE AND ANTON REPANICH

123

This was the end of the communication between the American Repaniches and the Vis Repanić family. What reasons could there be?

Maybe the Yugoslavian government confiscated further communications. Maybe, because of Anton and Winnies' frequent moves, the post office did not forward letters. Maybe, after the request for guns during the cold war, Anton decided to end the communications. Some on Vis remember a notification of Anton's death in 1972.

John's recollections of the stories lingered in the back of his mind. When he finally had a chance to travel, he had to see who was still on Vis... We fell in love with the island, bought our house and....so here we are.

PART 3
THE JOYS AND CHALLENGES

THE HOUSE AT BARGUJAC IN 2000

CHAPTER 16
A REAL FIXER-UPPER

While we were in the USA Drago hauled out several truck loads of garbage from the house, trimmed fourteen years growth out of the pine trees and brush around the house and recovered it to a point where we could make some decisions about remodeling. We need to be there to make those decisions, so back we go in the summer of 2000.

We get off the ferry in Vis harbor and drive up and around the hill that rises behind the town to get to our village of Bargujac. We stop at the top of the hill to take in the view of the valley below, now green with the lines of vineyards. On the valley floor red and white striped pillars mark the corners of the former Allied airstrip which is now planted back to grapes as if nothing had ever happened. We pause by the cross memorial for the English soldiers then wind our way down the narrow roads to Lokva, the lowest point of the valley, marked by a falling down red brick building nearly covered with climbing vines. Behind the building is a small *lokva* (pond), the only standing water on the island. Pertinent notices are thumb-tacked onto the shuttered doors along with some notices of times past, or the black bordered papers announcing the death of someone in the area. There are always a few old ones that no one bothered to remove. At this intersection we take the left turn rather than the right turn which would take us to Dračevo Polje. At Podstraža we turn right towards the sea. The tall, wispy grass on both sides of the narrow asphalt road brushes both sides of our car as we drive from the small village of Podstraža to the seaside village of Bargujac on the southeast side of the island.

The access into our half acre lot goes across another half acre lot which is for sale for $25,000, but we are told it is in the "green zone" and is not approved for building. Eta has assured us that the rocky, steep driveway is available for the use of this lot during construction. We tell ourselves that one property is all we feel like gambling on right now, so we pass on the idea of buying it too. *(Five years later, the owner is certain that it will be in the building zone and the price has skyrocketed to $300,000. Ten years later it is NOT in the building zone and the right of way is considered ours.)*

.

The designer of this house had not heard the American real estate mantra of "light, open and airy". The cement gray colored walls have never seen a paint brush. The living room of this fourteen year old, two story house looks out to the "million dollar view" through six glass doors that all open into the house leaving two square meters for furniture in the center of the room. A step up from the living room and through a narrow open archway is the tiny viewless dining area, barely big enough for a table with four chairs. The plumbing in the adjoining kitchen is against the back wall with no view to the sea. The opposite wall turns the kitchen into a tunnel that opens to the "summer kitchen" outside living area with a waist high fireplace for the sole purpose of grilling fish.

Behind the living room is a bedroom with no closet. *It seems that closets as part of the house are an American thing.* This bedroom has no window, but another glass door to the ground floor terrace. This door also opens into the room. *If you open the door for ventilation at night, who knows what kind of critters could walk right into the bedroom....and would a queen sized bed even fit in here? Many questions!!!!*

A good-sized room partially plumbed for a bathroom is across the short hallway. Two steps up the dark, narrow concrete stairway is a closed doorway. The irregular steps change direction with pie shaped steps around the corner making it nearly impossible to move furniture to the upstairs.

On the second floor is another large living area with the same awkward glass doors opening to a small terrace surrounded by a rusty metal railing. The larger upstairs bedroom boasts a spectacular southeast view to the sea through an aesthetically pleasing six-foot diameter circular window. It is hinged along the center so that the top half of the circle can be opened into the room and then lowered to the down position to open the window. *That is, if you happen to have three strong people to lift it down and if you don't put a bed in the room. This is not going to work.* Again there is no closet, but a loft area above the stairway. A non-descript bathtub stands alone in the bathroom. It must have been too heavy to carry out, as it was the only fixture left in the whole house. From the ceiling in every room a single light bulb dangles down from a wire sticking out of the grey plaster.

The entire house is concrete block and concrete from the floor to the red tiled roof. Curiously, on the roof there are three chimneys with charming little red tiled roofs on them. One goes to the summer kitchen fireplace but there are no fireplaces, stoves or even holes for stovepipes for the other two chimneys. *Curious!* The terrace is covered with a mosaic of various colored, irregular shaped pieces of marble, granite and white stones and bordered by concrete flower boxes sporting bright, happy looking red geraniums which have survived regardless of the neglect.

Irregularly shaped pine trees with trunks growing at every imaginable angle frame the "million dollar" view of the open Adriatic Sea. On the right, about one third of a mile out, is the green, brushy island of Ravnik. Its smooth curves remind John of a sleeping "Shmoo". On the back side of Ravnik is the famous *Zelena Spelija* or Green Cave. The white rock border along the sea stretches out to a long rocky spit pointing to Budikovac Island on the left, a favorite mooring spot for yachts. The parade of sailboats, yachts and fishing boats is never-ending in good weather.

The path from the house to the sea takes about fifty steps down a shady path, past rock terraces and piles, through the pine trees to the solid but irregular rocky shore and the clean, clear turquoise sea. Red molten flows, crystal formations and the remains of ancient stalactites are evidence of some ancient caves in the geological history. The soft limestone has been eroded over the eons to create a very interesting coastline.

We carefully measure the house so that John can make some drawings on the computer and we can plan the remodeling project. The cement walls in the kitchen and dining area will be the first to go. We will change the small pie-shaped interior stairs, and add a landing with a door to the outside and stairs down to the terrace. The rotten wood doors and windows will be replaced with vinyl sliders. Most of the plumbing and electricity will be upgraded. Drago tells us that we should add another underground concrete sewage tank. I doubt this system would pass the California permit process, but he assures us this system is safe, and judging from the cleanliness of the sea, he is probably right. We make plans to add a garage and while we are at it we decide to make a second floor apartment for our guests and to rent to tourists. Drago's response to every change is "*Nema problema*".

NEMA PROBLEMA

DESTRUCTION PHASE OF THE VILLA

DRAGO PREPARES CONCRETE

CHAPTER 17

NEMA PROBLEMA

We make three trips to Vis during 2001. John's American cousins, Virginia and Chuck join us in the spring for a shopping spree and progress check. Drago arranges for us to stay in an apartment in Vis town over the small food market next to his apartment building, across from the ferry dock. From the window which must always be open to catch the few breaths of moving air, we are part of the warm springtime nightlife of Vis. The generator on the ferry rumbles all night. A guy with a very noisy motorcycle shows it off again and again, gunning it as fast as he can right under our window. We are awakened (that is if we had slept) at 5 am with the loading of the ferry. The fumes from the diesel trucks waft into the room, along with the clatter and chatter. This is not the best location on the island, but it is very handy to the ferry and the little market.

On the shopping trip to Split we explore the only three building material stores that we know of. We quickly choose toilets, lights, shower fixtures, appliances, tile, gutters, beds, couches, and armoires. We purchase what becomes Drago's favorite tool; his "Hilt machine" or what we would call a jackhammer. Our neighbors sarcastically refer to it as "his constant companion". It must have been raucous while we were gone. *NEMA PROBLEMA.*

We come back to Croatia in June with our college friends, Liz and Jim. We pick up the furniture that we had ordered in Split and come to Vis in our newly purchased Jeep Cherokee (more about the Jeep saga later). We hurriedly put furniture together to have a place to sleep. Our comfort air mattresses have not yet arrived in a container from the USA. We feel very smug about our purchase of two L-shaped, dark green velvety couches with one lounge side, that make into double beds. These were the only "hide-a bed" type couches available. We did have a choice of blue or green cut velvet material. Our kitchen and one bathroom are marginally functional. We do more shopping for patio furniture, a television, and kitchen equipment. This is rather fun after 40 years of using the same stuff. It is somewhat like getting married and setting up housekeeping all over again, only this time with a little more money, no hand me downs and a totally foreign selection.

131

We soon find out from Eta that the government has denied the approval to own the property. Soon after we receive this bombshell information, John's citizenship approval comes through, but mine does not. Now as a Croatian citizen he can own half of our property. I was not approved to own the other half. *Then who does own that part if this is a community property country?* No one can answer that question. Eta calmly tells us that she didn't make the citizenship application for me, so I have to start over. A year and a half later it comes through, thanks to Nikola, the owner of the local pizzeria who knows the right person in Zagreb. The Croatian government allows the British to buy property in Croatia; Americans cannot. *Did someone tell us this important fact before we bought the place? Don't think so.*

On our last trip of 2001 (we are really racking up those frequent flyer miles) we drive to Zagreb with Drago and Rina to take their son, Stipe back to high school. Rina knows a few words in English and is quite anxious to use them. Stipe learned English in school and is our salvation.....until we leave him in Zagreb. Drago speaks some German and Zagorski (or northern Croatian dialect) which is quite different from the dialect on Vis. We start to understand that the language that we are picking up from Drago is a mix that not everyone can understand. *This could be dangerous.*

Somehow John and Drago have the same construction thought processes, and although the methods and measurements they have used individually over the years are completely different they have been able to communicate with each other from the beginning.

With Drago and John following all kinds of leads for vinyl windows, we have a great tour of the back roads, factories and little workshops of northern Croatia. We visit in Drago's relative's homes, eat unhealthy quantities of delicious meat, potatoes and fancy *tortes*, and thoroughly enjoy getting to know this area and the real people. At every stop we are offered coffee, wine or *rakija* and spend at least an hour visiting with the proprietors. Drago is much more familiar with this area than with Split. *I have never seen this particular tourist attraction on any tour advertisement. This is really up close and personal.*

Could we have done this on our own? Not on your life. Is it fun and interesting? You bet. And with Drago, everything is *Nema problema.*

When we return to the USA, we are still floundering about our future. Can we find another farm that will satisfy us? The answer is "no". Where should we live? Shall we build a house or live full time in an RV and travel around the USA? We tried that for a while and found it was not for us. We are thinking of our house on Vis as a vacation house for a couple months in the summer.

Our communication with Drago while we are in the US is by fax machine. Drawings and explanations spew out of the fax and we spend hours thumbing through our Hrvatsko-Engleski dictionary trying to translate them and to send responses back …in Croatian. We are amazed at how many words are not in the dictionary. Even when we can find the word, it doesn't necessarily fit the context. We kind of slide over those and the little words that seem insignificant. It turns out that the tiny word "*ne*" is very important, just like "not" in English. It sure can change the meaning.

It is just as well that we did not have a digital camera because the demolition pictures that we saw when we returned would have given us sleepless nights for sure. Drago keeps perfect track of every kuna and tries in every way to save us money. We do have some questions about an item on his bill every day for "Marenda". *Who is this girl who works every day?*

When we arrive on Vis in June of 2002 after a week in England with my brother, Bob and his wife, Diane, we find Rina, Drago and his worker friend from northern Croatia, Ljudva, anxiously waiting to see our response to the progress on the house.

The stairs and landing are changed and mostly tiled. The upstairs bathroom is almost complete with a corner Jacuzzi tub. The new sliding windows and doors are installed with "rollettes" and are a great improvement. *We now have room for furniture…….what a concept!*

They have put the pure white stucco, or *zbukanje*, on some of the exterior and dressed up the corners with stone trim. The new garage with the second floor walls is in process and it will just be a few more days to finish the walls. Rina has cleaned everything, planted flowers, and started a vegetable garden. We are totally impressed and reward Drago with a good bonus. "*Nema problema*".

Drago had asked us to decide whether we wanted a *beton* (concrete) roof or a wooden beam roof on the new garage. All of the collapsed roofs that we see on 200 year old houses have rotten wooden beams. We don't know much about concrete roofs but Drago tells us it is the best insulated and the cheapest and *nema problema* to build, so that is what we will have.

Our goal is to have the garage roof on and windows and doors in and enclosed by the middle of July when our guests will be arriving and before our neighbors arrive from Zagreb for their vacation stay in their small stone weekend house. We have no idea when they might arrive. Our effort shifts from a relaxed vacation mode to busy, work mode to finish the roof quickly.

The first step is a concrete beam all around the perimeter of the walls to hold up the special rebar and red tile "*greda*" that span across from side to side and hold each other up in the center ridge. There is lots of shoring up with long boards from the concrete floor/ceiling below.

Ljudva, Drago, John and Matko hang the special tile blocks in place between the beams that will hold up the concrete. The honeycomb style holes are great insulation. These will serve as a base for the four inches of concrete.

I perceive one big *problema*: the roof is up on top of the second floor. How do we get the concrete up there? At this point there are no ready-mix trucks or pumps on the island, so concrete is all mixed at the site in small mixers and transported in wheelbarrows. Just about everything is built with concrete. Drago suggests that he might borrow a *diselica* in Vis. We can not imagine what a *diselica* is, but it is some kind of elevator. We find it is not available now so Drago and John "engineer" and build a ramp from materials that are around the yard. We are glad OSHA is not here to judge its safety. *Nema problem.* Ljudva and Matko set large pre-made rebar mesh over the roof blocks. This roof will be STRONG.

The 3rd of July is the day to pour the concrete for the garage roof. We start at five in the morning with Ljudva, Drago, Stipe, Matko, his father and three other young men. Four men shovel the sand/gravel mix and cement into the small mixer. John notices early on that they are mixing a stronger mix than Drago had told him, but Drago says "*Nema problema*", it will be strong. Two strong young men run repeatedly up and down the steep, narrow ramp to the second floor roof. One guy is pulling the wheelbarrow by a rebar handle, and the other is pushing and steering by the handles. Drago and Ljudva smooth the concrete on the roof and John keeps busy sweeping the rocks and spilled cement off the ramp, although all the workers assure him that is not necessary. "We do this all the time".   Drago insists, *"Nema problema."*

The crew stops at 7:00 am for a little liquid refreshment of beer and/or travarica, a strong brandy. Rina and I prepare kielbasa sausage, cheese and lots of bread to serve at 9:30 am. We need to adjust our eating times, to include *"Marenda"*, the on the job meals which Drago brings out, Rina cooks and we pay for. *So "Marenda" is not Drago's girl.....but a mid-morning meal served to the workers.* We clean up after *Marenda*, and then load the oven with eight pounds of pork ribs for lunch and heat up the already hot house.

About the same time John comes in to tell me they are out of cement, and need twelve more bags to finish. *Problema*! He asks, "Will you look around the neighborhood to see if there are any bags to borrow until we can have more delivered this afternoon". I walk around the neighborhood looking for cement mixers or piles of cement. Every house has a cement mixer stored somewhere. I find a young teenage boy near a cement mixer that is running and ask if he knew if they had any bags we could borrow. He speaks good English and takes me to his grandfather, who also speaks English. He has one extra bag that I could borrow, but I cannot carry it back. *What a way to meet your neighbors.* When I return I find that John is on his way to Vis to buy cement. It is important to finish this pour at one time while we have a crew.   John returns with the cement and the crew is back to work. My mind flashes back to our walnut harvests; the necessity to finish quickly, the frustration of a crew waiting on the clock, the intensity of the job. The difference is that our harvest crew always brought their own lunch and didn't drink alcohol before nine in the morning (or ever on the job).

The last wheelbarrow of concrete is pushed up the ramp. The crew ceremoniously raises the Croatian flag on the top of the roof, and sings a workman's version of the national anthem, a tradition on every new roof. WE FINISHED THE ROOF JUST IN TIME. Our neighbor, another Maja, arrives for her yearly two-week stay. The garage will block her previous view to the sea which was peering through our dining room and living room windows. They could have a great view, but they prefer to leave the pine trees to block it. Maja's reaction was that it was going to be very nice, and that we can work together to make the yard beautiful. *Okay !!*

The crew finishes around 2:30, eats lunch and are all gone by 4:00. In a week or so they will put on some insulation followed by the typical red Mediterranean tiles. *NEMA PROBLEMA!*

CONSTRUCTION OF OUR CONCRETE ROOF

CHAPTER 18

FERRIES and SHOPPING IN SPLIT

Vis is 30 miles from the mainland of Croatia and 60 miles from Italy. It requires a two and a half hour ferry ride from Split or one and a half hours on a faster passenger catamaran. During the tourist season the Jadrolinija line runs three trips each way on a large, modern ferry, but the winter months are a different story.

In the first few years, we get up at 4 am to catch the 5:30 am ferry to Split. John and I go upstairs to the miniscule non-smoking cabin on the ferry, Lastovo. The first ten people into the "salon" have already stretched out on the natty velvet, maroon colored upholstered benches to sleep, leaving only a few chairs for latecomers. Most of the passengers sit at tables in the large smoking section, drinking their first small cup of the blackest, strongest coffee imaginable and smoking. Drago sleeps in his truck in the "garage" lower deck.

We arrive in Split at 8 am. Most of the stores open at 9 am and close at noon for the afternoon rest when everyone eats their main meal. They reopen at 5 pm to close at 8 or 9 pm. The afternoon ferry returns at 4:30. This gives us three hours out of a twelve-hour day to shop. If we know where we are going (on our early trips we had no idea), we might get half of our list accomplished. Street signs are almost nonexistent and are only on the corners of some of the buildings. The street names all sound alike to us: *Vinkovarska; Vukovarska; Vukosova; Vukosoviceva; Vitazoviceva*

By the time we find a street sign and read each letter to be sure it is the right word, we have forgotten the name of the store. Stores and offices are hidden in the corners of an alley, on the street floor of an apartment building, or upstairs in a grocery store. They have minimal signs.

One of our first trips is in Drago's two-seater truck that is bigger than an American full size pickup but smaller than a 1-ton truck. He doesn't have any better idea about the layout or locations of things in Split than we do and is learning right along with us. At least he speaks the language. My designated seat is in the middle over the hot engine on a pillow or blanket. John's excuse for taking the outside seat is that his legs are too long and would get in the way of the center gearshift. Seat belts? Who needs them? Air conditioning? Non-existent. Europeans have much more tolerance for close traffic encounters than Americans do. More than once I thought we were going to run over a pedestrian or another car. No one seems to notice.

One large building materials/house wares/hardware store is a superb example of how to discourage shopping. At the entrance the only choice is to go upstairs into the house wares and lighting departments. Occasionally there is a cart at the top of the stairs to use while shopping. Today there are none; they are all downstairs. The only way to get downstairs to get a cart is to go down a ramp at the far back corner and go to the front of the store. I find a cart which I push to the back corner again to go up the ramp. A clerk gives me a sign with her forefinger waving from side to side indicating that I am not supposed to take it up the ramp. What do they expect me to do? How do they get the carts up there? I take it up anyway. What can they possibly do to me? The only toilet is in a small room obviously for the workers. The sign on the door indicates that it is not for public use. I always have to go "right now" when I get to the far corner of this store. I don't ask. I just use it. Poor lighting, dirty merchandise, and worst of all, no available rest room give me good reason to hate going here. Most other stores are clean and pleasant and have restrooms.

We do have questions about some of the merchandise. Why would anyone want to buy a toilet with a flat platform in the bowl that needs to be cleaned every time with the ever present toilet brush? The position of the flush lever on American toilets is fairly consistent, but the Europeans make it a game by changing the position on every model from a pull chain too high to reach, to a little faucet handle to turn on and off. I guess it does add some intrigue to an otherwise ordinary task. What is the purpose of a bidet? Every store clerk insists I need one to match my toilet. No one tells me why.

Light fixtures in Croatia are similar to fixtures in America. But where are the ceiling fans? In this warm Mediterranean climate doesn't it make sense to move the air a little on a hot, still day? We have exactly one (1) choice in fans; It is a fake glitzy brass color with four ruffled little glass light shades sticking out to the corners, a little plain round globe in the center and fake wood color blades that are reversible to the wicker look. This must be the original ceiling fan design. I'm not an interior designer, but I know these fans will look bad in any room. How can I integrate these with a modern, casual design? Even after they are installed, the Croatians turn them off because they can't stand moving air....anyplace.

Do Europeans ever have more than a tiny load of laundry? Do they always dry their clothes on a line? It must be so, because on a sunny day drying clothes wave from every apartment balcony. Why does it need to take one and a half hours to wash three bath towels? That is all that will fit in a typical European front loading washing machine. I buy a combination washer/dryer and find that it takes about 4 or 5 hours to complete a wash and dry cycle. I join them and hang up everything outside.

Have they never heard of a garbage disposer? I want to buy a slow cooker or crock-pot. The Dalmatian cuisine would adapt very easily to it. Their diet has very little fried food, but there are twenty different models of deep fryers in every house wares department and not one crock- pot.

Maybe it is just because I am used to the American system of filing papers, but it seems to be much more efficient than slipping each paper into a plastic page and filing it in oversized three ring binders that are stacked on shelves. By the way, the ring spacing is different in Europe and so is the paper size. I started with the European method but as soon as I could get a filing cabinet here, I changed.

Taking the car to Split is expensive, so occasionally we have opted for walking or getting around by city bus. The first few times we tried to get around in Split by bus, we could find no maps or schedules and our Croatian language skills were very bad. We have learned the system and the bus company now has printed maps and schedules. Now it only takes us about 10 minutes to decide if we are waiting in the right place. When we discovered the directory, Total Split, our shopping trips became almost efficient. With maps, bus schedules, English and Croatian language indexes of categories, this "yellow pages" is our constant guide in Split. If we call ahead with our mobile phone for directions we quite often have someone from the store come to meet us to show us the way and occasionally to give us a ride back to the ferry dock. People are friendly and very willing to help....but they don't seem to recognize the difficulties for strangers in their city.

In ten years we have seen enormous change in Split from the three building supply stores we could find in 2000. Now, several large modern shopping centers and super markets have sprung up and seem to have good business; and they stay open all day and part of the evening. Most of the little old cars have been replaced with newer little cars thanks to readily available, but expensive credit. Ten years ago, we could only find one furniture store.... Now they are everywhere. There is even a decent selection of ceiling fans.

Hvala Bogu (Thanks to God) Split's beautiful old center stays the same with Roman history oozing out of the stone columns of Diocletian's Palace. Small classy tourist shops make for interesting tourist shopping. Just down the street toothless, wrinkled grannies, dressed in black skirts, black stockings, with scarves covering their heads, still hawk their fruits and vegetables in the large buzzing green market. The aromas of the fresh fish market fill the air until noon with a fantastic selection of amazing sea creatures. Visitors and natives alike enjoy having a cup of coffee in the sunshine on the beautiful Riva while they watch the ferries come and go. No doubt about it....Split is a beautiful city.

CHAPTER 19

GETTING AROUND

Tiny, vintage Yugos, Zastavas, Renaults and Volkswagens in various sun worn colors with rusty edges make up the island auto population. At harvest time they pull a little trailer and they become the harvest trucks, full of baskets of just picked wine grapes bouncing to the konoba where they will be pressed into wine, or olives on their way to the press. In the winter they are piled high with the prunings from the vines being transported home where they will be used as fuel for their outside grills. There is no place on the island to drive over 40 mph, so these mini autos fit right in with the laid back, slow, *polako* lifestyle. They could fit into the tiny, scarce parking places in Vis town and they could squeeze around the hairpin turns without crossing the line; but they do not. Many of them find a way to take up two parking spaces and both lanes. Most of theses cars never leave the island and find their final resting place pushed into a corner, covered with weeds where they just rust away until the occasional scrap truck comes to carry them away.

If we are going to have a house out of town we need a car to get around. On one of our early trips cousin Joško had arranged with his friend and restaurant owner, Andro Slavić to find us a car to rent while we are on the island. When we arrive and ask about it Andro nonchalantly tells us, "The man who owned the car took it to Split for a few days. But don't worry; you can use my car when I don't need it." We manage to fit into his schedule and get along fine. Now there are many rental cars available.

****

When we venture out on our first car trip in Europe, it becomes quite clear to us that driving in Europe can be a challenge. There are just too many tasks for one person to handle at one time. It takes four people to deal with map reading and operating the GPS, understanding signs in a different language, narrow twisting hilly roads, drivers who have a totally different threshold for speed and space, taking photos out the window and sightseeing. Why should we have to think about shifting gears? John vows to buy an automatic transmission car to get us around on the island and to tour around Europe.

Drago suggests that we stop in Germany on one trip and visit his cousin, Ivan, who owns an auto repair shop in Siegen. Ivan knows everything about cars and will help us find a Jeep Cherokee. We track down a few leads, have a wonderful tour of the German countryside, but don't find the right car. We enjoy the gracious hospitality of his wife, Paula and his two sons. Paula works two jobs and never stops working when she is at home.

The next attempt to find a car is in Zagreb. We had traveled from Vis with John's American cousins, Virginia and Chuck, in a rental car. Sandra and Bruno, our Croatian friends who had saved our bus ride on our first trip, take us to the "only place to buy used cars in Croatia". We find ourselves at the Zagreb fairgrounds on a Sunday afternoon. There are hundreds of cars for sale, organized by category and make, with anxious owners ready to pounce on potential buyers. We find three cars out of the hundreds with automatic transmissions. One is a Jeep Cherokee that looks to be in good condition. When we show some interest a young man with a ponytail starts his pitch in English, takes us on a test drive and tells us it had belonged to the wife of someone in the American Embassy. *Yeah. Right!* To prove he has the registration and to get us the information we needed, he accompanies us to the bleak, gestapo-feeling police station in Zagreb where we wait in line for a couple hours and never get to the right person before the office closes. *Wouldn't you trust someone who took you to the police station to get the registration? We do.* He offers to rent it to us for a week to try it. Our "legal advisor", Eta suggests by mobile phone, that we should have some kind of contract signed and notarized. That is not possible on a Sunday night so we ignore the advice. We drive the car back to Vis, use it for a week then return it to him in Rijeka after we discover we cannot get registration for it because we are not Croatian citizens. *Why didn't someone tell us this at the beginning?* Later Eta found out the car had been stolen and if we had been caught with it we could have been in big trouble. *Ooops!!!*

Our next step is to try to decipher the Croatian language want ad magazine, <u>Mali Oglasnik</u>. Once you learn the abbreviated lingo you can buy just about anything from this weekly publication. Every so often an automatic transmission car is listed. Just as we are ready to head back to the USA, we see an ad for a Jeep Cherokee with American registration located in Dubrovnik. As Americans we could own this one, so we arrange to look at it when we return in a few months.

Apparently, there is not a big market in Croatia for an American registered car because it is still available when we return.

With our college friends, Liz and Jim, we return to Split and drive a rental car to Dubrovnik to check out and to buy the Jeep. The seller has arranged for a great room in the old town for us to stay for the night and a guided tour of the Dubrovnik area. The next day we drive off in our 1997 Jeep Cherokee with expired FLORIDA license plates which never fails to turn heads and bring out exclamations of "FLOREEDA!!!! How did you get it here?" usually followed by a loud guffaw as the vision of the Jeep floating across the Atlantic Ocean crosses their minds.

A couple great weeks traveling to Slovenia, Austria, Hungary and Poland with Liz and Jim convinced us that Vis is a great place to use as a base for European car traveling. The only problem we encounter on this first venture into Europe with our own car is discovering at the Austrian border that our car insurance is good only in Croatia. We pay dearly for insurance to drive across Austria. The other countries don't care and we don't know any better. Lucky for us we didn't need it. *We sure do have a lot to learn.*

In the summer of 2003, when we both have our Croatian citizenship and it is okay for us to own a Croatian car, we decide to take the necessary steps to complete the process of registering the Jeep.

We drive to Northern Croatia to meet Drago's cousin Ivan again. Ivan had been visiting earlier in the summer in Vis with a different woman. Now he is coming from Siegen to Lepoglava to his retirement house with his wife, Paula and his sons. He is bringing headlights and four new tires for the Jeep to bring them to European standards. *We are not sure if it is up to or down to European standards from American... just that there are different requirements.* Drago, who has been in Germany, rides to Lepoglava for 12 hours on a dining chair in the back of Ivan's van full of furniture and used appliances that Drago will take back to Vis in his truck. The buzz is that the "other woman's" husband had just hung himself in the woods in Germany. I wish I knew the whole story on this. It sounds like a real soap opera mess, complete with a suicide note. We take Drago to Varazdin to get his truck, and then back to Ivan's to load it with the stuff that they brought from Germany. John and I drive to Ivanec to get the tires mounted.

Drago and Ivan grew up in this area. Drago's father, a pleasant gentleman, was hanging around most of the time. Now we see where Drago got his fun-loving personality. Drago and his dad did not speak to each other for a few years for some unknown reason. Drago even changed his last name, but now they are back on good terms.

In the late afternoon some village children are playing badminton in the yard. John finds a couple tennis racquets and hits the ball back and forth with them. We show them our English/Croatian flashcards that we have been making and they learn a few English words. In the evening Ivan straps on his accordion and everyone joins in the singing. What is it about this oompah music that gets to me? I sing along without knowing any of the words. *Nema Problema…..Oh, my…now I'm saying it all the time.* After a sweaty, long, day we are ready for a shower before bed, but the town is on water rations—off at 10:30pm and back on in the morning.

The next morning John and Ivan install the lights on the Jeep. It is not quite as simple as they had planned, and it requires a trip to an auto junk yard to get some connectors. The children are back hanging around until I start to pay attention to them. Since John is busy with the lights, I play games with the flashcards with the kids for a couple hours.

With our new lights and tires, we head off with Drago to the neighboring town of Ivanec to start the process of licensing the Jeep in Croatia. Drago gives us a paper with the title HOMOLOGACIA. Part of the application process for Croatia to join the European Union is a requirement for Croatia to bring their cars into compliance with European standards. *Boy, do some of them have a long way to go.* We know also that we must have a technical inspection and go through customs to "import" this car. We do not understand the process, and apparently no one else does either. The technical inspector informs us, "We must first go to customs". The customs officer asks for our purchase contract and calculates in his head that we must pay about $11,000…..more than we paid for the car. He tells us, "You must go to the technical inspection first".

It is not possible to do any business between noon and four pm, so Drago takes us to his *Teta* (Aunt) Mica's for lunch. Our experience from last year was that we would eat way too much. We were right again. After we eat a week's calories for lunch in the house we all walk up the steep hill to the weekend house where the family is grilling enough meat for a restaurant. *Teta* Mica loads our car with wonderful canned pears, pickles and some liqueur that is for "women only". Back to Ivan's to sleep. No water...no shower again.

The next morning, John and I arrive again in Ivanec at the customs office when they open at 8:00 am. No one speaks English there, so we call the main office in Zagreb to find out what we need to do. No one seems to know the process. We decide to start driving to Zagreb and go to the office in person. On the way to Zagreb we call our friend, Sandra, to see if she has any ideas. She suggests that since we were near the Slovenian border we go to the customs and technical inspection there, so we turn around and head to the border. Thinking we needed the technical inspection first, we find that station and are ready for the inspection, but they insist, "You must first get a declaration of customs at the border." At the border, they send us to a *Spedicia* office that can fill out the papers for customs. None of them can do it for us there since the car needs to be licensed in Split. We decide to drive the six hours to Split to be at the customs office there in the morning. We arrive in Split around 1 in the morning and sleep in our car at the ferry dock.

We are at the customs office when they open. We are directed to a young man who speaks English; a good soccer friend of John's "cousin" Siniša. He and his boss, (another friend of Siniša's) assure us that the customs charge will be based on the present value. They will do all they can to help us. But first, we must get the inspection.

At the inspection station, an English speaking insurance man takes us under his wing, looks at our papers and tells us what we need is not the normal inspection, but a *homologacija* inspection, verifying that our car meets European standards. The inspector motions that our new headlights are good, but there is no European stamp on the tires. We must have new window glass all around. WHY? John's patience is waning. He asks the inspector to call his boss and get an exception. The inspector disappears for a few minutes then comes back with the decision. "They will approve the windows, but we must get tires with a European stamp." *These new tires must have the stamp, but where is it?*

We make a call to Drago for advice. "*Nema Problema*. We

should drive to Dugi Rat, down the coast about 20 miles, (an hour or more in tourist traffic) to get the inspection. Talk to Igor down there and tell him you know Drago from Vis." Igor is on vacation, but comes over to do our inspection. He also is concerned about the tires. We finally get Ivan on the phone. He thinks maybe the tires were installed backwards and we should look on the inside. John climbs underneath and there is the stamp.... but, this inspector will not make an exception for the windshield glass. Back to Split. We show a different inspector the stamp on the tires. He calls again to get the exceptions for the glass and gets it. *Does anyone understand the system?*

To pay for this part of the process I get directions to go to a magazine stand across the street for some tax stamps, then around the corner to the bank in an inconspicuous corner of a large, communist style apartment building to pay and get a receipt. Apparently this is to avoid under the table payments. As I stand outside in line with about ten people in front of me pouring out the door of this tiny bank, John's voice comes in loud and clear on our walkie talkie in English. "Do you have the papers with you?" He had given me the wrong papers and was coming to get them. Everyone grimly and silently glances my way as if I was going to rob the bank.

The man who had been helping us brings John in a car to get the papers that he had mistakenly given to me. They speed away to the post office to pay. I have no idea what is going on. We expect the inspector to give us the final papers, but now he says we cannot finish until the seatbelts are changed. The seatbelts are marked "made in Mexico". A wonderful young English speaking woman in the office who is waiting for service, steps in to help us get across the point that they are standard and that we are not going to change them as no one seems to know the difference between Europe standards and American standards. *Since we had already paid, we think he was in a pickle and somehow, he decided that he could make an exception and signed and stamped the papers. Whew!* Later we found the mark, which would have made the seatbelts pass the muster.

By now it is too late to go to customs, so we drive to the 3:30 ferry, come home and jump in the sea. That plunge into the warm, clear, clean, turquoise water reminds me that the tranquility of the sea is why we will endure these human inadequacies and bureaucratic mazes to be here in this place instead of some easy chair. It is just another interesting challenge.

The next morning, we are on the 5:30 ferry to Split with Drago. We go straight to the *Carina* (customs) office to finish the customs part of registering our car. Siniša's friend calls a Spedicia worker to help us get the paper work for customs. We give her the information, and then wait for about an hour in a coffee bar for her to call us. They verify the serial number and model of the Jeep and then calculate what we need to pay. Altogether it totals half the cost of the car. This is a very high taxation, but the best solution at this time. We had already investigated the possibility of shipping this car back to the US and buying one already registered here. Buying a Croatian car, which has already gone through the customs process, is even more expensive. We will look at it as our contribution to their economy and go on.

Did you think that was the end of the process? Not quite. We had to go through the annual technical examination of every function of the car. This inspection is held for two days each month on the island. Every one of these little old Yugos and Zastavas must pass this annual test to renew their license. How some of them pass is beyond me, but the system seems to work. I wonder how many payoffs slip under the table. The Jeep passes this thorough examination which includes the inspector driving down a steep hill to test the brakes. *I guess that is one way to do it, but what if they fail?*

We must now take the papers to the police in Vis to issue the license. That involves going to another magazine stand for tax stamps, to the bank or post office to pay a receipt for registration, then back to the police for the registration book. Then we must take the old Florida license plates into Split to trade them for Croatian plates. Unbelievably, we finish the whole process in less than two months.

WHO FORGOT TO GET THE RIGHT OF WAY?

WELL, IT IS 90% FINISHED

CHAPTER 20

TWO-METER AUTOBAHNS

In 2002, we stop to let a car go by on the "two meter wide autobahn" that leads to Bargujac. A crew of young Croatian soldiers is blasting rock and cleaning weeds on one side of the narrow road. *If you ask me, it is a good use of the young men who at that time were required to do two years of military.* When we ask one of the young soldiers what they are doing, they tell us they are widening the road from the valley of Lokva to Milna, the village past Podstraža. That is great news. At that time if two cars met, one of them would have to back up to a wide space. At least now there will be room for one car to just pull off onto the scraped area. For three years nothing else happens on this road.

Then in 2006 a grader scrapes off one meter of grass and a machine cuts off about a half meter of the edge of the old asphalt and lays it down in a narrow row. New asphalt is laid one meter wide, up to the row of old asphalt...but not enough for two cars to pass. In fact, now we have a net gain of half a meter with a hard pile of old asphalt to jump over if we should happen to meet another car. This situation remains for another year.

In 2007 we see a new sign that announces the modernization of the road. We see road building equipment parked along the side of the road and evidence that they scraped off the weeds one more time. Are they actually going to finish the road? I guess not. Along the road are several crude, homemade, hand painted signs warning: *NE ÐIRAJ-PRIVATNE POSJED* (DON'T TOUCH-PRIVATE PROPERTY) with lines spray painted on the ground to mark the very small pieces of private land that the owners are declaring will not be part of the road. What happened? Did someone forget to get permission or pay for the right of way from the landowners? Are these pieces being held hostage for a better deal?

In the spring of 2008, the contractor is making serious changes cutting 20 foot deep cuts through the highest hills, straightening out the curves and leveling off the hills and valleys. Along side the new road are mountains of crushed rock. Finally concrete gutters, culverts and asphalt are laid before the tourist season, making a first class highway. A few NE ĐIRAJ signs remain and so a few short one-lane stretches remain in the middle of this great highway. *We have observed that most government projects are completed to about 90%. Here is an example of the 90% rule.*

★★★★★★★★

The two lane road coming out of Vis winds up the hill with a few hairpin switchbacks and then down to the valley with more switchbacks. One day we notice forty-four new posts along the side of the road from Lokva to the top of the hill. We cannot imagine why they are installing so many. On the next trip, each post going up the hill has a bright yellow sign with red arrows to mark the curves. Some point to each other and some actually stick out into the road. *This is overkill!* Going down the other side, there is just one sign at the top warning of curves for the next few kilometers.

★★★★★★★★

The winding, narrow roads snake around the various hills of Vis, from village to village. The road maintenance crew seems to be one white-haired, wiry man armed with a weed-eater, pick and shovel. He alone cleans the weeds off the rocks and around the small concrete barriers and cleans the drains. Chemical weed control is out of the question on this *prirodno (*natural) island. Occasionally a mechanical mower comes out to give him a break where it won't run into a rock wall.

★★★★★★★★

On a beautiful, clear day when my brother, Bob and his wife, Diane, are visiting we decide to take a picnic lunch to the top of Hum, the highest point on the island (about 1800 feet). We notice on the way up that a crew had paved part of the road, but all the paving equipment is parked and no one is around. We set up out folding chairs next to the tiny, stone Sveti Duh (Saint of the Spirits) chapel. We spread out our lunch of prsut, salami, cheese, bread and wine. We gaze through the binoculars to the coast of Italy and then on the other side of the hill, to the mainland of Croatia. We marvel at the view straight down the hill to the town of Komiža. We make up stories of Roman soldiers placing

150

rock piles in an intricate geometric pattern on the hillside; or are these messages to alien civilizations? We watch as paragliders float over the island and the sea like birds.

After a couple hours we head down the hill and walk up the steep rock steps to Tito's cave where he spent time during World War II. We notice that the paving machine is working below us and taking up the entire two meters of road width. This could be a *mala problema.* A woman and man are measuring across the road, so we ask them, "How can we get around?" They answer that it might be an hour or more. We drive down close so they won't forget about us and take a little snooze while we wait for them to unload the asphalt truck. We see that they are stopped and several men have their heads under the engine hood. Out comes a large broken fan belt, and we know we are in trouble. There is an old stone guard tower on one side and a four foot drop on the other side of the road… no way for even our Jeep to get around. The workmen are unconcerned about us. We watch the rather interesting proceeding for a while with the binoculars, then get the word from the roller operator that they are waiting for a new fan belt and a mechanic to come on the ferry that leaves Split in two hours and it will take three hours to get here. *No use waiting here. My clever brother comments, "Be it ever so humble, there's no place like HUM."*

As we walk down the hill, five more trucks full of hot asphalt arrive on the scene. All the asphalt comes hot from Split on a special ferry. We walk up another hill to Zena Galva to our friend, Darko's agro tourism restaurant. He says he has no food today, so we decide to try out his neighbor's new restaurant. We sit at a table under a huge tree. By now it is dark; dinner time in Dalmatia. A small lantern in the middle of the table lights our delicious grilled lamb dinner.

We are not too far from Dračevo Polje, so we call Joško and explain our problem. He drives to the restaurant, discusses the situation with us and the lady owner who had offered to take us home or to the car later. Joško and John go to see what progress has been made and find that the paver has been repaired and is working again, but we will not be able to get our car out until they spread the five truckloads of asphalt.

Joško, an active promoter of island tourism, is very angry that the asphalt is going on this relatively unused road to the military

151

outlook, and not on the local roads that have been waiting for paving for thirty years. John tells him, "Don't be angry about the asphalt. This gives an easy road to the top of Hum for tourists to view the beautiful panoramic views. You just need some"panorama"signs pointing up the hill." Joško grumbles and offers to take us back to Bargujac.

John waits at the restaurant for Joško to return, watching the dishwashing procedure (all washed and rinsed in the same water) and fly control. A large hanging pot in an unused fireplace has a piece of meat or fish inside which has attracted all the flies during the day. A direct spray of RAID right into the pot takes care of the pesky flies which fly out in a buzzing cloud and die.

Joško and John watch the action on the road from Joško's house across the valley. John arrives home with the Jeep around 12:30 am. *A great adventure!!! The next time we went up the hill to Hum, Joško's handmade sign pointed up the hill to the "Panorama."*

CHAPTER 21

JUST TRY TO MAKE A BUSINESS

Watching one family's quest for economic independence has provided an insight into the challenges an entrepreneur faces when trying to start a business in Croatia or Vis. Jerina's neighbor, Dobrilka, has been a good friend from our first days on the island. She has retired from the business world in Zagreb and is always ready to translate or explain some Croatian system to us in English. She lives on the Riva in the building that was the first hotel in Vis, owned by her grandfather. When we first meet her, she and her mother live together on the ground floor in a large room, always rather dark with the windows all shuttered.

Add to the scenario, her daughter Tihana, a recent graduate in history from the University in Zagreb, who wants to make a life and a living on Vis. They turn their small garage into a laundry service for the tourists and yachters who stay the night in Vis Harbor. When they recognize that tourists bring in their laundry in the late afternoon and want it washed, dried and ironed before morning, they give it up.

Dobrilka and Tihana sell us a parcel of land to finance a beautiful remodel of the stone building into a first class restaurant in a prime location with living quarters upstairs. They hire a chef and waiters and wade through an immense amount of red tape to open a restaurant.

Enter Tomislav, a husband for Tihana who will manage the restaurant. They live in constant stress and fear of the government inspectors who will inspect their inventory and sales to be sure that every item that was purchased has been used or is still on the shelf. The recipes and menu items and prices must be approved by some bureaucracy in Split. Nothing can change without approval. They measure portion sizes to the gram and they must account for the number of servings they sell. They can't use a fresh tomato from a neighbor's garden without a receipt and certification that the seller is a registered business. This is a nightmare, but they are dealing with it and doing okay.

153

A baby girl, Josipa, is added to the family to make four generations of females and Tomislav living together over the restaurant. Tihana has a special artistic gift and thinks a high class gift shop of items all made in Croatia would be a great addition to the restaurant. They rent the adjoining space and open the gift shop. Tihana does very well selling these quality items by giving each customer a story about the item. Tomislav manages the restaurant and Dobrilka cares for little Josipa and her mother.

One day I stop in for a visit. Josipa is over a year old and is always in her playpen or stroller. I ask if she is walking yet, and the answer is "only by holding my hand". I comment that I think she probably is able to walk alone. Tihana reluctantly takes her out of the playpen and sets her on the floor. Josipa immediately starts running alone from one side of the room to the other clapping and laughing out loud, falling a few times and then getting herself up to run again. Tihana is crossing herself and holding her arms nearby to catch her. Finally Tihana relaxes and then says "this is the most exciting day since Josipa was born". I am surprised at the extremely overprotective mothers, but I understand. They do not have a toddler friendly environment. They live in a small apartment on the 2nd floor with steep stone stairs. Their yard is the Riva with no barriers to the sea; a far different environment from American carpeted homes with fences all around. I tease them now that Josipa at age 6 would still be in her playpen if I hadn't rescued her.

With an active toddler and an elderly bedridden mother who both need constant care, Dobrilka can't help in either the restaurant or the gift shop. The hired clerks for the gift shop don't try to sell anything, but just sit at the cash register and wait for their paycheck. The sales go down. After a couple years they close the gift shop. The city of Vis charges exorbitant rent for the small outside seating area which is an ideal location for a summer tourist restaurant. They have the same problem in the restaurant, which they close the next year.

The lesson to them is that they have to run the business themselves because employees don't care and cost too much in taxes and benefits. The government regulations seem unrealistic and unmanageable. I wonder who is benefiting and how does it help the economic growth of Vis and Croatia? The restaurant closes, the city gets no rent, and Tihana and Tomislav go to work as employees in another restaurant and hope something better comes along. End of story? I hope not.

TIHANA AT HER RESTAURANT
A PRIME LOCATION ON THE RIVA

CHAPTER 22

DEALING WITH THE SYSTEMS

As I walk along the Riva in Vis town one morning I stop by the glass covered bulletin board outside the meat market to read the lists of names of the "parties" that will be running in the election for mayor and town council next week. There are about ten parties, each listing ten names. We can vote for one party or list. We recognize some of the names and it seems that the good ones are all on different lists. When we ask people that we trust about the election they throw up their arms and make a motion like "get rid of them all."

When we try to register to vote in the city hall, a lady tells us that the registration is closed, and they have no way to know if we were registered. *How can they not know who is registered?* On Election Day, Sunday, we walk up to the Podstraža *Hrvatski Dom* polling place to see if we will be able to vote in the local election. Each village has one of these cultural centers built by the Yugoslavian government for a meeting place. The local government maintains some of these two story buildings and others remain boarded up eyesores. We take a folder full of documentation and are prepared to hear that we are not registered. As we walk in the door, the election official calls my name, "Patricia", hands me a paper ballot, and tells me to circle the number of the list I want. They do the same for John. Each "list" is from a political party and has some candidates that we would vote for, but each list also has some candidates that have been identified by friends as "old communists" that want things to stay the same. *We are hopeful that a more democratic, forward-looking government will win, but we have no idea which "list" will accomplish this.*

If a party or "list" gets a majority, then they choose the mayor and have a majority on the council. This election does not produce a clear majority, so the parties try to make a coalition government. The main function of the governing body will be finishing the *Prostorni* (land use) Plan. They cannot come to an agreement, so the Croatian government appoints an interim mayor until they can have another election. Land use planning is postponed.

At the next election, there is still no majority, but they have an ultimatum from the national government that they must form a government. No one seems to be very happy with the new council. Because these are mostly new people with different interests and different cronies, the Land Use Plan will probably have to start from scratch to satisfy the new interests. We don't hear anyone who trusts the politicians. Several young people have told me that politics is the only way to make money.

We had been involved in local politics and land use planning as farmers in the Sacramento Valley in California. Planning is always controversial and pits developers against environmentalists, farmers against environmentalists and farmers against developers. No one is ever completely happy with the whole plan, which is why it works in America. We have learned to live with majority rule and compromise. It is a public process with input from the people.

In this fledgling democracy, many of the old guard leaders are still at the helm with their communistic ideas, but with new titles and some new laws to deal with. Now, in 2011, the new mayor is interested in talking to the citizens and is doing a good job for Vis. Entrance into the European Union is the number one priority for the government. Corruption is still part of the system, although they have to show the EU that they are trying to bring corruption to a reasonable end in order to join. A striking difference that I notice between America and Croatia is that in America we are very aware of our elected representatives and have easy access to their offices. The people I know here don't seem to know who the representative to the federal parliament is or feel that they have any input.

Drago uses the word *"mafia"* freely, always with the gesture of stuffing one's pockets. Anyone who puts extra money in his pocket or charges too much falls into the dubious category. We have been told that in the judicial system, the various parties pay the judges before the trial. *I assume that whoever pays the most, wins.* Our neighbors have had a law suit with some relatives about the use and ownership of the parcel next to us, for thirteen years with no hope of ever coming to a conclusion.

Since 2003, there has been a moratorium on building anything new on the island. One plan came down from the Vis government for public viewing and comment, and then disappeared when the Croatian government decided that all plans for the islands must be consistent.

Each new mayor and council will look at all the "deals" made by the old council and probably make their own "deals". The new plan is very secret, and is always promised for "the new year" or "the end of the month", or "next month." The public will not have input until it is published. One can only imagine the controversies that will arise.

****

A large World Wildlife Fund poster on our wall proclaims that Vis is one of the "Jewels of the Adriatic" and states their purpose:

"Stretching down Croatia's coast, the Dalmatian islands have been identified as one of the last pockets of paradise in the Mediterranean by WWF. The archipelagos of Vis-Pelagruza, Lastovo and Mljet are still almost pristine and have the richest biodiversity in the area, home to both an impressive range of natural beauty and cultural heritage. But, the potential for damage is huge, as a surge in mass tourism is already affecting the Croatian coast. With the country expected to be one of the top destinations in the Mediterranean by 2020.

WWF is working with Sunce, a Croatian environmental association, and with all local stakeholders to preserve the biological diversity of the area, initiate sustainable use of natural resources and develop responsible tourism."

At the end of 2007, there is still no *prostorni* plan, but at the beginning of 2008, there are maps that can be viewed and disputed. According to these maps there would be very little new development, and no new building within 150 meters of the sea in the "green zone". There are a few areas designated for tourist activity. Two hundred letters of protest are turned into the city hall, given to a consultant in Split and, as we understand, returned with all of the requests denied. The council will decide the fate of these properties. In 2011 the main plan is finished, but they expect it will be two more years before the municipal plans are finished and ready to give building permits.

This moratorium is not helping the economy of the island. The island is already 50 years behind the other islands and the coast because of the military occupation. No one is sure which property will be in a building zone. *Our property is all legal and now grandfathered in to the plan, so up goes the value of our property.*

Renovation of the old buildings is permitted and goes on. If all the old, empty stone houses on the island are renovated, it could push the infrastructure to its limits. Every day there are truckloads of building materials arriving on the ferry. Where are they going?

****

A foreign investor put out about $6 million to purchase an old, unused factory building in a prime location on the Riva in Vis and a defunct sardine cannery in Komiža, which comes with some beautiful beaches. His intent is to construct environmentally friendly tourist facilities to benefit the island residents. He had to guarantee employment for about forty former cannery employees for three years. He tried, unsuccessfully, to find work projects for them on the island, such as grape harvest or cleaning beaches. The bureaucracy blocks any good ideas for their productive employment—so these non-working employees just pick up their paycheck each month and then have the gall to demand vacation pay. If he fires them, he must pay all the remaining three years of wages to them in a lump sum. For more than five years he has not been allowed to pursue his plans. In 2012 the old factory building has been renovated and is now a campus of Vern University. The sardine factory is used as boat storage.

****

One evening, we hear a man call out, "Repanich?" We respond, "Yes" as he enters our open back door. He explains that he is collecting the garbage bill for the city of Vis for the whole year (about $30). He has a stack of papers for everyone in the neighborhood. This is the most friendly bill collector, but we are happy to pay because we get frequent garbage pickup at the top of our driveway.

We get our water bills handed to us occasionally by a neighbor whose wife works in the water company.

If the postman sees us, or a neighbor, on the road or in town, he will give us the mail for the neighborhood.

The doctors may be out making house calls, so the office hours may not be consistent. *Yes, you read that right....House calls.*

CHAPTER 23

FORTY YEARS OF BELONGINGS

Once we decided to live on Vis, down sizing and parting with farm tools, supplies, scrap metal, building supplies and personal items accumulated over forty years of farming in the USA is a traumatic and emotional experience for John. Luckily, the Croatian government allows citizens returning to Croatia to bring their personal belongings back into the country one time without a customs charge. *I'm not sure how we possibly qualify for that category, but we do.*

Things from our large storage building in California are designated to one of four places: a huge dumpster, a container to go to Vis, a semi truck to store in the USA, or to a huge garage sale. Our philosophy is "if there is a chance that we may need it and can't buy it on Vis, pack it in the container." When John packs, there is no room for even a mouse to stowaway.

Our friend, Fred, has been to Vis a couple times and wants us to have his extra sailboard in the container for him to use when he comes again. He delivers the sailboard and sees that John and I need more help loading the container. His long legs and arms reach into corners and he jams in more than John thought was possible. The cost of shipping the container is based on volume, not weight, so anything that fits, goes in our twenty-foot container. John and Fred find a place for lots of tools, nuts and bolts (American...not metric), pipe, some boards to use for shelving in the garage, his favorite welding table, a cherry-picker hoist he had made, Lazy-Boy chairs, a radial arm saw, a metal 4 x 4 box of unused bricks, scaffolding, etc. I add some of the American conveniences that are not available (or too expensive) in Croatia....Ziploc bags, peanut butter, sheets for our queen size beds that we had shipped earlier, an American filing cabinet and supplies. Aunt Winnie, before she died, asked us to take her clothes to the women in Vis, so boxes of clothes are stuffed in.

We make three trips into Split, to three different offices, to get the paper work completed before the container arrives. We must translate our container inventory into Croatian and the values into kunas, and get a notary to write a letter to the customs office verifying the contents. The tracking program on the computer says our container is on its way to Italy, and should be in Croatia on June 13. It will then take a few days to get it to Split. When we go to the fourth office to present the papers to claim the container we find that the time for arrival of the container has changed to after June 17th. *Why doesn't that surprise us?* On Wednesday, June 23, we call about our container and find that the shipper in the USA has changed the final arrangements here. The new agent knows that the container has been delivered to Ploce, Croatia on Monday. *Nice that they let us know.* The US agent didn't send the bill of lading or information that we already paid for the shipping from Ploce to Split. After about 10 people pass the buck, we email, fax and phone our agent in the US. He is very apologetic and promises to correct everything. We have heard nothing since Thursday.

On Monday, June 28, we learn that all the papers have now arrived. It is back in the hands of the original agent and we can come get it. Tuesday, we go into Split with Drago and his truck. The truck is just in case we have to take something out. We arrive at the Spedicia office by 8 am. The truck with the container arrives around 9 am with our 20 foot long container in the middle of a 40 foot long bed. The Spedicia office prepares the papers for the customs officer who wants both doors opened. *We silently pray, "Please don't ask to see everything because it will be impossible to put it all back in".* She sees our hoist and asks if this is for a business. (Our one time exemption for paying customs is for personal belongings...not business things.) We assure her that it is part of John's personal tools and that we are not starting a business here. She says, "Close it up". We breathe a sigh of relief as she presents the bill, but she says something to Drago and he tells us to add some extra kunas to get her to sign off. *It is the system.* We pay an exorbitant amount to bring the long truck on the ferry.

Drago has arranged for us to unload the container at the old winery on the way out of Vis where there is good security and a loading dock. Dario and Dinko Repanić and the local forklift help unload onto the dock in four hours in the evening so the truck can return to Split on the morning ferry. With six of Drago's truckloads and three Jeep loads, we get it to Bargujac. *John is ecstatic that he still has part of his farm, and now we get to organize it AGAIN.*

162

CHAPTER 24

A HUNTING MEN WILL GO

Dinko is a serious hunter! John has casually enjoyed hunting in the USA over the years and wants to join Dinko on Vis. In Nevada it takes John three minutes and $35 to purchase a hunting license at Wal-Mart. He never had a trained hunting dog on our farms. Our family pets loved running and tracking pheasants and thought they were pedigreed hunters. Hunting for the pheasants and rabbits on Vis is not as simple. There are no other wild animals on the island, unless you count the cats that roam around looking for a handout.

The Croatian government regulates hunting. A hunting club manages hunting on Vis following government regulations. They select members, elect officers, collect dues (around $150 per year), and work to maintain the pheasant and rabbit population of the island. To hunt on the island you must first apply to the club and pass a vote of members (*sounds like a fraternal organization to me*). This vote is just permission to apply for a license to hunt. Gun ownership and registration is another matter.

John has his US hunting license translated into Croatian. He sends the translation with proof that he has been accepted into the Vis hunting club to an office in Zagreb for final approval. Four months later he receives notice that he will have to pass an examination on hunting regulations, the history of hunting in Croatia, and ethics and all the animals and birds that can be hunted. Since there are only rabbits and pheasants on Vis, that part is easy. The text that he purchases to study is all in Croatian. The "professor of hunting" from the University in Split will give him the examination. *Who ever heard of a PROFESSOR OF HUNTING? From the University no less!* Dinko and his granddaughter, Sandra, help John study before the test. Dinko says, "It is all common sense. Don't worry about it". *Common sense in English is one thing.....common sense in Croatian for John is a totally different concept.* The examination is scheduled for the first of October, but then rescheduled for around the 20th or 21st. Of course, this year's season is already underway. *I wonder if they are making up rules as they go along.*

We go into Split to meet with the Professor of Hunting for John's examination. He spends about five minutes speaking with John in English about the pleasures of hunting on Vis, signs a document that John has passed the examination and *to je to* (that is that).

John takes his signed "final" paper into the Vis police station. Next he must bring in his "diploma" from hunting school, along with some passport photos. A few days later he receives his "diploma" in the mail. It is about 15x18 inches, on parchment type paper with a muted hunting design in the background, with hand done calligraphy. *It is nice enough to frame, so it occupies a place on our living room wall.*

We make another trip to the police station with the "diploma" and two passport photos. Now they give him a list of additional papers that he needs to bring in and the address and phone number of a doctor in Split that he must go to for a physical examination. He calls the Doctor's office in Split for an appointment. They tell him that he must go to the doctor in Vis before he comes to Split. The Vis doctor gives him an EKG, and various tests. He takes the results into the Split clinic. They say that the Vis doctor was only supposed to send a letter and they do all the tests again, along with an IQ/spatial relations test. John passes all of their tests and takes his results to the police in Vis. The police give John the permission to own a gun. *Now this is real gun control!*

John has a favorite shotgun that is at least forty years old. He brought it in a special case on one of our trips before we recognized the problems of registering or owning a gun in Croatia. USA airport security inspected it carefully. At the Split airport no one was in customs so we just went on through and took it to our house. Now we learn that without the permission to own the gun the police could have confiscated it at the airport. *OOPS!*

To register this gun he must provide proof that it has passed customs, a receipt and serial number. This old gun has no visible serial number and a little searching on the internet confirms that it never did. *Will the police believe that? They want a receipt for a gun that John purchased in 1965 from a friend.* We know that we don't have an original receipt here (or anywhere) but computers and scanners can do unbelievable things and John now has a receipt for his gun. He sends it and an email letter that verifies that the gun has no serial number to the translator in Split for official translation. The police accept both of these.

Getting the gun through *carina* (customs) is a different problem. Dinko knows a man who works in *carina* in Split who comes to Vis every weekend to fish. He has offered to help us. To get things started we offer to pick up the "custom's guy" at the ferry to take him to Komiža and talk to him about how it could be done. He suggests that we bring him a fish. *I don't get this. He tells us that he will spend the weekend fishing, so why would he want us to bring him a fish?* I bring him some homemade cookies instead. He says he will think about how he can help us and if we pick him up on Sunday to take him back to the ferry he will have an idea.

When we pick him up again he lays out his plan. We are to send a package from the USA that looks like a gun, and put on a label that says "GUN". He outlines what should be in the package: certain CDs, (he would let us know which ones) some Levi's in his size, some sweets and other things that he would suggest. He will intercept the package and keep whatever is in it. In turn he will give us certification that the gun has passed customs. As he gets out of the car he asks, "Where are my cookies?" as if this was a requirement. Then he tells me, "I prefer cookies with cream in them". *That's enough of him. We'll find another way to get the gun through customs.*

We take the gun to the airport. We explain that we did not find anyone in customs when we came off the plane and now realize that we should have declared it. We don't mention that it was a few years ago. He tells us to bring them the gun. John walks into the airport with the gun in a pipe case. They inspect it, and then take about an hour to write up the papers. They send us next door to the airport police who call the Vis police department to find out what they told us. They take another hour to figure out how to fill out more forms. The duty is only about $25 (the original cost of the gun 40 years ago). Now we have 8 days to take it to the Vis police for the final permission to have this gun. This time the police tell us to pay $7 at the bank and get $12 worth of the little tax stamps from the newsstand, and bring the receipts in the next day. *That's it...mission accomplished.*

Hunters must have a registered, pedigreed, hunting dog with a diploma? Apparently dogs in Croatia can only hunt rabbits or pheasants.....not both. Bach, named after Johann Sebastian, is

165

Dinko's pheasant hunting dog. He lives chained to a doghouse, as do most other island hunting dogs. Bach is used to devouring the scraps from the hotel dining room. Since Dinko retired from his job as procurement manager from the hotel, Bach has had to change his diet to mostly dry bread scraps from Dinko's kitchen.

To hunt rabbits, the hunters must go in pairs with their trained dog. One hunter goes along with the dog to scare up a rabbit. The other hunter waits by the road (usually in a chair) for the rabbit to run by when he can shoot at it. John doesn't call that hunting and besides we don't really like these rabbits to eat. Mima was Dinko's rabbit dog, but he sold her. Now he wants her back, and asks John to buy her back. John agrees, and now they have a rabbit dog. *So why are we helping with the rabbit dog?*

A few weeks later, Mima is not eating and looks like walking skin and bones. We are taking the car to Split, so Dinko takes her along to the vet, as there is no veterinarian on the island. The vet suggests Mima should be in a hospital environment rather than chained to her outside doghouse. I, with a lot of sympathy for the dog, agree to bring Mima to our house for a few days to see if we can keep her warm and get her fattened up. The blood tests won't be back until later. We are repainting the living room, so we have only one couch out. We set up a box with an old blanket for her and carefully cover the couch with a large piece of styrofoam at night. The next morning we find the styrofoam on the floor in a million pieces and her blanket neatly placed on the couch. *Who is in charge here?* A couple weeks of pampering, and Mima goes back to her normal environment, tied up to her doghouse.

The blood test results say she has an incurable condition caused by sand fleas. She does well during the summer, but with the cooler weather she goes back to her poor condition and dies just before hunting season.

Ivica, from Rukavac, is the neighborhood "chairman" for hunting. He comes by every so often to get something…a passport photo, (*I think we have given them three*), some money, or to explain John's job to keep water in a few locations for the summer months for the pheasants in our area. John asks him about practice shooting. Not allowed.

On another of his frequent visits, he explains in the fastest

Croatian possible, the new limits and regulations. Each hunter can take one male pheasant each hunting day, up to six for the season and one rabbit for the season. I can't believe that anyone would keep a pedigreed, trained dog chained up all year so that he could hunt one wild rabbit. The hunters will be required to keep track of each animal they take, so they can survey what they have (or had) for animal populations.

When Dinko comes out to make plans with John for Sunday opening hunting day, he explains that the six pheasants and one rabbit limit per season is just a tax evasion thing and that no one was expected to stay within the limit. It seems that the hunting club pays a tax to the government according to how many animals are reported.

John leaves before dawn to meet Dinko for hunting pheasants. If it has not been clear before, I should explain the unique terrain of Vis. It is a series of high hills and valleys, which over 3000 years of history have been totally covered with rock wall terraces and rock piles. Now these walls and terraces are covered with brush; rosemary, heather, small pines, blackberries, etc. Dinko and Bach don't go horizontally along the hill sides to hunt. Instead they go from the bottom to the top of the hills, up and down the rock walls. When Bach finds a pheasant, the dog and the pheasant play a game of out-staring each other. They can wait up to five minutes for the pheasant to finally get spooked enough to fly out. At least that gives the hunters a little rest while they wait. When John suggests the familiar American system of the dog immediately flushing out the pheasant, Dinko explains that would ruin the game for Bach. *Can't do that now could we?*

On another hunting morning, a lady from the Hunting Ministry from Zagreb meets with all the hunters at the beginning of the day at the little red brick building at the bottom of the hill at Lokva. As the army of hunters stand around leaning on their guns, this official lays out the new regulations. She assigns the hunters to groups of six to ten to hunt with the "special" dogs for the rest of the day. *What is the purpose of this? We have no idea.*

Each hunter is supposed to donate a pheasant for a door prize at the "Hunting Dance" that will be in February. John takes one of his cleaned, frozen pheasants (just the skinned breasts and legs) to Ivica's house. He is not there, but his wife gives us a very strange look, and takes the pheasant. Ivica arrives at our door one morning with our frozen pheasant package. It seems we were supposed to donate a whole pheasant. We don't know exactly what they want so we drive to Dračevo Polje to ask Dinko. He pulls one complete bird out of his freezer, (*feathers, head, tail, guts and all*) for us to give to the Hunting Club for the dance. *I don't believe it.* Dinko says he doesn't like to eat pheasant anyway. He doesn't like to clean them and gives them all away. All of the pheasants at the dance were whole, frozen uncleaned birds, and those who won them were thrilled. *We will still clean our pheasants before they hit the freezer.*

TYPICAL ROCK PILES AND WALLS WHICH COVER VIS

DRAGO AND JOZO WITH THEIR CATCH

DRAGO PREPARING THE FIRE TO GRILL FISH

CHAPTER 25

VIS CUISINE

I have come to the conclusion that anything that grows on the island or in the surrounding sea is edible and probably good for whatever is ailing you at the time. During the lean years, folks lived off the land and the sea, eating fish, sea urchins and shellfish, young lambs and goats, all sorts of weeds, herbs, wild mushrooms, etc. At any time on the island there is something to be gathered…wild asparagus, capers, snails from the land or the sea, mushrooms, certain weeds for salad, fruits from wild bushes, rosemary or oregano to dry and sell, wild garlic, etc.

FROM THE SEA

John discovers that the new watch he bought is a "fishing watch". *I think that is something akin to a Lone Ranger decoder ring for big boys.* He has been researching how it predicts the good fishing times. It shows hour-by-hour 1 to 4 fish depending on the prediction. It is all about the sunrise and sunset, moon stage and rise and fall, and tides. He determines that 5 am on Friday, June 15, 2007 will be a four fish day, the best time all year for good fishing. The new moon rise and the sunrise will be happening at the same time. He works hard on Thursday to get the boat in the water, so he will not miss this optimum moment for a 4 fish day. We are up at the crack of dawn to give it a try.

We cut four perfectly good squid into one inch squares, and wrap them around the seventy hooks on the *parangal,* a long fishing line with the hooks hanging down with nylon leader. They all fit into a plastic tub which holds the line with a rubber piece with slots around the top for hooks. The sea is perfectly calm (*bonaca*). This line is let out hook by hook, (my job) as the boat moves along (John's job). The line is held between two floating jugs which are tied to long ropes with a rock anchor on the ends. The idea is to leave this baited hook line for a couple hours, then come back, carefully pull in the line, take off the fish and the bait, then replace each hook and line in the bin slots. It looks easy when we watch the locals do it, but it just takes a little pause or tangle (my fault) to get it wrapped around the propeller. *We won't do this again together…the two tiny fish we snagged aren't worth divorce.* Someone forgot to tell the fish that this was the optimum time, so they are all still safe in the sea. Our neighbor fishes alone every day with nets and or *parangal* and sells us his extras. *Those are my 4 fish days. We should have grilled the squid.*

****

We are on an excursion with Drago in his boat. On the way home he strings some strips of calamari on his fish hooks and throws them in the water just off the shore. He has no fishing pole, but nylon line wrapped around a swiveling handle. Drago says he must be 5 meters out from the shore. He continues at a good speed and in about 30 minutes has caught 6 fish for our dinner. We figure that it is cheaper to pay Drago to go fishing, than for us to buy fish in a restaurant.

****

Near our dock, we have put out this chicken wire contraption with some old bread for bait. One day we discover a large ugly critter in this fish trap. We identify it in the fish book as a Mediterranean Moray eel with large, sharp teeth and an aggressive behavior. *Oh... this is interesting. Call Drago.* Drago is excited to see this "*Marina*" and when he brings it in, he knows just what to do with it. He takes a large stick and beats it over the head, then sticks a sharp knife through its head to be sure it is 100% dead, and then proceeds to clean it. Our granddaughter, Monica asks about all the parts of the guts and handles them to see how they work. Drago grills him for us. It is a very mild flavor and delicious. *Monica, however, eats pasta.*

****

Our grandkids love to catch small octopus in nets while they snorkel. Again, Drago is our expert. First he turns the head inside out and removes the guts. It is then boiled along with a couple of potatoes. When the potatoes are done, the octopus is done. Let it cool; cut it into small pieces to make a delicious salad with the potatoes, garlic, parsley, a little vinegar and olive oil.

****

Vis men grill fish in outside fireplaces over a fire of grape prunings burned down to perfect coals. Seasoned with native rosemary, lots of olive oil and garlic, it is always wonderful. At lunch time in the summer, the aroma of grilled fish is the aroma of Vis. According to

172

Rina, the best part of the fish is the head. Her pleasure is obvious as she sucks the juices out of the head and eyes. She asks our 11 year old grandson, Alex, if he can eat fish eyes. He answers," if you can, so can I," and ceremoniously sucks out the eyes.

FISH ON THE GRILL

Everything from the sea that doesn't go on the grill can go into brodetta, a delicious and always unique fish stew. With onions, tomatoes, olive oil, and white wine there are a few rules that must be followed. According to my Croatian cookbook, the brodetta cannot be stirred, only shaken; you never add ground pepper; it must be uncovered because even a drop of water from the lid can ruin the sauce; and when cooked over a fire, don't add new wood. It is always tasty and can be a challenge to eat, depending on what is in it…fish, mussels, octopus or lobster. It is worth it.

****

Every special event calls for the speciality of Vis: Pogača or fish pie, a two crusted baked yeast dough filled with salted sardines, and sauteed onions. If it comes from Komiža it has tomatoes, or if it is from the Vis side of the island, no tomatoes. It is a perfect picnic meal for eating in the field during grape or olive harvest. Don't miss it if you come to Vis.

GRANDSON ALEX ENJOYING THE WHOLE FISH

We take Rina and her friends to the nearby island of Ravnik in our boat to pick capers, the tiny unopened buds of the exquisite caper flowers. These plants grow near the sea in the rocks and out of walls all over Vis. I try picking for a while, but decide it is not productive enough for the small amount of capers I will use. It is always hot and there is no shade. The plants are all on the ground on rough terrain. This is not for me. The gals pick for several hours and get a small basket full, which will be hand-stemmed, cleaned and put in jars of salty water, then sold to tourists.

The thousands of nesting seagulls on the island are letting us know we are not welcome on their island. What a racket!!! We see only a few young ones as they are mostly still on the top of the island in the dense brush. If we even looked like we were walking that direction, the mamas and papas flew at us, coming pretty close but never touching us. I guess they haven't figured out that a better defense would be dropping on us. If they tried, they didn't have very good aim. *Hvala Bogu.* (Thank God).

Wine production is a tradition… not a business. We arrive at Dračevo Polje to help with grape harvest at around 8:15, have coffee with Joško and Vedrana, and then walk down the rocky drive to the vineyard. The crop is bountiful. We cut and drop heavy juicy bunches of white Vugava grapes from the vines into buckets, then pour them into large plastic boxes which Josko stacks in the back of his little Yugo to deliver to the cooperative in Podspelia. Here they are weighed and tested for sugar content.

At noon, when the crop has been delivered, we walk up to the little stone house for lunch. Vedrana has prepared sardine brodetta and Josko grills fresh sardines. We break small pieces of bread into our bowl, and then pour some of the brodetta broth over it. We eat it along with our grilled sardines. Of course Josko serves some great red Plavac wine that he siphons out of his large barrel. It is customary to dilute the wine with water to make *bevanda*. When we help harvest the red Plavac grapes, they go to his konoba where Joško makes the wine for himself and family.

KONOBA MOJA, which translates to MY WINE CELLAR, was one of the first Croatian songs I learned. Everyone sings along to this song and I understand why. They love their cool, stone walled konoba on the ground floor under their stone house. It is where they make and store wine and artifacts of times before. They all love the song, the wine cellar and the wine. Most of the small vineyards on Vis are lovingly cared for by the retired couple of the family with help from the younger generations on the weekends when they come from Split where they work or attend school. It is a tradition, and to some a hard fast rule, that in July and August no one enters the vineyards because disturbing the vines during the hot weather will cause them damage or disease. The vineyards have been in the family for generations. Unfortunately only a few families actually make a profit from the famous, wonderful wines, which have been renowned since Roman times, but many families make enough for the family's consumption. It is interesting to us that the bare land that is available for wine growing on the island is more expensive to buy than the best irrigated farm land in California that is planted to permanent crops.

It is customary when you visit a Vis home for them to offer their selection of homemade liqueurs. These liqueurs are made from the distilled rakija or grappa with added flavors from every imaginable source: walnuts, almonds, certain grasses, koromač/anise, figs, roses, sage, lemons, cherries and on and on. The base rakija must come only from Vis grape skins. The flavoring ingredient must come only from certain sources only on Vis. Everyone knows the recipes and the strict rule for every kind is that it must at some stage sit in the sun in a glass jar for 40 days. I wonder what happens if you leave it a few extra days or cheat and take it in early. Some of these liqueurs are for women, and some are to go with certain foods. Each one cures something. *Most are amazingly good and some are pretty close to rocket fuel. Be careful!!*

I must add a note on *Orahovica,* the walnut flavored liqueur. It is made from immature walnuts, still inside a green hull. As walnut growers in California, we had never heard of a walnut liqueur and had no idea that the nasty green hull, a major disposal problem, could be an ingredient in a super liqueur with inumerable health benefits.

JOŠKO MAKING WINE

176

OLIVE OIL

This is what I have learned from Vis locals about *maslinova ulje,* olive oil: *Olive oil is LIFE. Without olive oil, we could not live. You can never eat too much olive oil. Using any other oil will shorten your life for sure. Fish must swim in the sea, then in olive oil, then in wine. Olive trees are the most precious plants in the world. Everyone should have a few olive trees in their yard. Olive oil from my field, my island, my country, my continent is better than any other in the world. The way I prepare my olive oil is the best way. Any other way is inferior. Everyone else adds regular vegetable oil to the olive oil so it is not pure. Mine is 100% pure extra virgin. Soaking olives in sea water before they go to the press makes the oil better. Soaking olives in sea water is a terrible idea. I will pick olives on Vis until I am too old to stand up. You don't ask children to help pick olives. If you use a little plastic rake which makes it easier, you get too many leaves. Each one must be picked by hand and dropped onto a tarp. You must remove every stem and leaf before they go to the press. A few stems and leaves won't hurt. The best place to socialize during olive season is at the cooperative press.*

We agree to help Dinko and Joško with the harvest for a couple days. We join Dalmatia's over 65 population under the olive trees. I have always considered olive picking to be the lowliest job in agriculture, but here I am enjoying the sunshine and gabbing with Sandra about her university experiences. It is not hard work, but kind of a challenge to get every last olive off the branch. We load up our car with the harvest and deliver it down the road to the press where someone has brought a pogača for everyone to enjoy. At lunch time Dinko starts a little fire in the field and we roast sausages. The second day he prepares a great grilled fish lunch. We are rewarded with enough oil for our use for the year and really have a great time. It is just enough of a reminder of our farming days.

VEDRANA WITH A BAG OF OLIVES READY FOR THE
PRESS

****

Vis women have standard recipes that they stick to and most don't experiment much with food. *Blitva* or Swiss chard is usually cooked with potatoes. Artichokes are cooked with large peas until they are overdone. *Bob* beans (big soft lima beans) are the most important plant in the garden. We plant sweet corn seeds from the USA, or we would never eat really tender, fresh corn. The same goes for green peas.

****

We hear Beep, Beep, Beep! If it's Monday, it must be Cica with his mobile farmer's market. On Wednesday it is Lupi and on Friday it is Vesna and Tonči. The three produce vendors that sell in the outdoor market in Vis in the morning drive their vans full of fresh fruits and vegetables to the villages to sell their wares in the afternoon. It is a time when neighbors gather to share news. I love it. Although the selection of produce is not as extensive as Safeway, the quality and freshness and most importantly taste is beyond compare.

TONČI, A VEGETABLE VENDOR, DEMOS HIS
SAUERKRAUT

FROM THE FIELDS

Dinko brings a bag full of almost tennis ball size figs from Draćevo Polje that are light green on the outside and like pink jam on the inside. Delicious. We eat as many as we dare and put the rest to dry in the sun. When they are dry I take them to Jerina's to learn how to make them into the *hib* or fig cakes that we like so much. We grind them in a meat grinder, add *koromać* or anise seeds that grow wild here, then mix in *rakija*, the distilled grappa. We shape them into four 6 inch round cakes. Now I must dry them some more on fig leaves turning them every day.

Drago brings out a couple boxes of what look like crab apples. He shows us that you only eat the ripe (black, mushy) ones. They do taste okay, but it's a little difficult to get used to eating what looks like rotten fruit. He warns us not to eat too many. Don't worry.

Vis citrus fruit is the best. We get fantastic mandarins from September through January, and then oranges and lemons decorate the island trees all winter. No one would think of spraying them even if they needed it. We enjoy fresh orange juice all winter, and lemonade from frozen juice cubes all year.

****

IF WE CAN'T GET FISH, WE WILL SETTLE FOR MEAT

How many ways can you cut meat? The cuts available here have little resemblance to American packages of meat. Many are cut with the grain. At first I had to "moo" to let the butcher know I wanted beef, and pat myself on the rump to let him know what part of the cow I wanted. One store now has packages with a picture of the animal and an indication of where the cut comes from, so I have fewer surprises. Pork and great veal are easily available. Beef isn't quite the quality of a good American beef steak. Meat here is classified by whether it is for the grill, the oven, soup, or *kod peka*, (under the bell).

Lambs are butchered as little babies. They are very tender and tasty if you can find the meat. When we raised sheep in Washington state years ago, we could not sell a lamb under 90 pounds. These little guys are about 30 pounds.

AT DARKO'S KONOBA, GRANDSON NATHAN FEEDS
A LAMB, WHICH MAY BE SOMEONE'S MEAL TOMORROW

I must have ruined *marenda* one day when Drago brought out a slab of what looked to me like bacon, but it had a label calling it *hamburger*. Looking at the fat, I decided it had to be cooked, so I sliced it and fried it for the workers to eat with fried eggs and fried left-over potatoes. When I put it out, Drago asked if I had left any of the *hamburger* uncooked. *With McDonald's all over the world, doesn't everyone know what a hamburger is? It is not this stuff that looks like bacon.* He explained that they don't cook this meat and they also don't eat cooked left-over potatoes. *WHAT?* I quickly came up with pasta to replace the potatoes and the rest of the uncooked fat meat.

****

Our grandson, Nathan, on his first visit to Vis when he was four, was afraid of Drago. In Croatian, *drago* means "dear one", but to a four year old American boy, the word, drago conjured up visions of a dragon? Add a big, heavy man with huge arms and hands, a toothless grin, and a strange language and you have a monster to a four year old. Nathan soon recognized that the honey on his toast was amazingly good and that the fried eggs we fixed for him were better than any he had ever tasted. We showed him that Drago's bees made the honey from the wild flowers on Vis, and that Drago's chickens made the wonderful fresh, brown eggs that he likes so much. One day he announced to Drago, "I like your honey. I like your eggs. I love you, Drago." They have been good buddies ever since.

YOUTH TENNIS PROGRAM ON THE REFURBISHED
TENNIS COURTS

CHAPTER 26

WHERE IS THE NEXT GORAN?

When Croatia's Goran Ivanišević won the Wimbledon Championship, he became Croatia's hero and tennis became the game that children wanted to play. John has always loved to play tennis and is not bad. With retirement came the opportunity to dust off his old racquets, and get back into it. In the beginning the tennis courts in Vis are barely playable, but we always plan some time to hit the ball around when we make a trip into town.

I am not a tennis player, but I don't mind trying to hit the ball back or run after John's serves for exercise. I love the ambience on the Vis tennis courts. I can hear a donkey "hee hawing" as he chomps the grass in the ancient Greek cemetery just off the corner of the courts. The church bells from three churches are signaling that the time is noon. On the day when the children from the island are receiving their first communion I think each of them is getting a turn pulling the bell rope. On one quiet morning the dogs from all around the town are barking as if they are conversing from one hill to the other. From a dozen outside grills wafts the tempting aroma of fish cooking over grape wood with the seasonings so special to Vis. Just outside the courts, the ferry prepares for departure.

****

When we return from a short vacation (*Aren't we always on vacation?*) we head to the tennis courts to find that they have been completely redone with new surfaces, nets, lights and seating for spectators. A Croatian Island Pro tennis tournament is planned for the next week with players coming from all over the world. Not exactly the US Open, but this should be fun. John volunteers to judge or help however he can. The local Vis kids are the ball kids and have a great time. At the end of the tournament the mothers prepare a huge table of traditional Vis cookies, dried figs, tiny fried fish, and of course wine, for anyone and everyone to enjoy.

Just after the tournament, a professional tennis trainer, Boris, volunteers to start a program for the Vis kids. He has these kids enthusiastically showing up on both days of the weekend and after school for lessons in two groups. Someone donated 10 tennis racquets, which they all share, and they have all the balls from the tennis tournament. John offers to assist him and has fun for a couple of weeks, when the program suddenly ends.

Shortly after the demise of the first program, Šime, a Vis native, starts a program for the kids again. John volunteers to help again. Šime has just finished a degree in physical education at the University in Split and has great ideas and the kids love it. He has about 50 kids signed up to pay 100 kunas ($20) a month which some pay and others don't.

The program takes four hours everyday, either in the morning or afternoon depending on the school schedules. Children go to school in the morning one week and in the afternoon/evening the next week, sharing the one school with the high school. I spend my time visiting friends and interviewing (*snooping*). It is great fun for both of us and a novel way to get to know the kids and their parents.

Šime explains to the kids that we have purchased tickets for some of them to go to Split for the Davis cup semi-finals. He explains to the group that they must have their parents' permission and that we could not be responsible for them all day. That doesn't seem to be a problem and the parents send their kids off for the day with us. There seems to be no concern about liability or that the kids might have any problems. *One little boy's father calls Šime asking what was going on because his son had come home and told him that he was going to be playing a tennis tournament in Split against Bosnia and that he had to go. KIDS!!*

We take the 7 am catamaran into Split along with six 12 year olds who are going to the Davis Cup with us. Šime finds a few extra tickets so they can all go to both matches. We all meet for lunch at a pizzeria, then walk ten minutes up to the sport center. The kids sitting with us were quite interested in the first match, but the others decided one match was enough and they all left for the 2nd match and found their way back to the 7 pm catamaran doing who knows what for 3 hours. *Every kid has a mobile phone and could check with Mom in Vis, and there seems to be no problems letting the kids go on their own.*

The second day 8 year olds, Ivan and Marin are with us from the start on the catamaran. We know these two boys are full of energy

184

and mischief. Šime again met us and we walked along the harbor to the marina on the west end for John to pick up a part for the boat motor. On the way Marin threw a plastic water bottle in the sea. I reprimanded him... he said "*nema veza*" or "never mind" ... After that whenever I saw a plastic bottle or other trash on the street, I had him pick it up and put it in the garbage. I called him my garbage man the rest of the day. I think he got the point. You can't take the teacher out of me.

Keep in mind that these boys don't speak English much beyond, "Hello, what is your name? My name is ------". I found out that Marin also could clearly say, "I don't like pizza with mushrooms." Ivan said "thank you" at every opportunity.

Šime married a Slovakian girl and moved away so the program fizzled, but for six years after this experience, the kids still come around the tennis court hoping to find John to play a little tennis. The parents still comment to us what a great program that was. *John's participation in the tennis program helped us to be acceptable foreigners.*

THE GRANDKIDS ENJOY SNORKELING FROM THE
DOCK

OUR SECOND BOAT SLIDES INTO THE SEA

CHAPTER 27

THE BLACK HOLE CALLED A BOAT

In the beginning, our rocky waterfront property presented a challenge for ingress and egress to the sea. But again Drago insists that it is "nema problema". With a few wheelbarrows of cement, some rocks picked up along the beach, and a lot of ingenuity he and John build a smooth cement dock that sits on the original rocks and blends in as if it was always there. He adds some easy steps into the sea, and we have a comfortable place to lie in the sun, and to get in and out of the sea. It also makes a great place to load a boat.

One look at the calm sea and the beautiful day tells us we need to go on a boat tour today with our guests, my brother Bob and wife Diane. Drago is working with us on one of our many projects and since we haven't found the right boat to buy yet, he goes back to Vis to get his boat for our tour. His boat has undergone many iterations and changes over its long life. I believe it was at one point a wooden craft, but by now it has morphed into a fiberglass coated tub. It has a framework that could hold a shade, but there is no shade. With a one cylinder diesel engine that is hand cranked to start, it has a sound recognizable for a long distance. Everyone moves to the edge of the boat while Drago leans his round body down to crank the motor.

The first stop is the Zelena Spelija (green cave) on the backside of Ravnik, the island in our million dollar view. Drago turns off the engine and we float silently into the cave. The sound of a motor would certainly ruin the ambiance. A four foot diameter hole in the roof of the cave captures the sun's rays in the middle of the day. A shaft of bright light shines into the water and dances in a sparkling light show on the walls of the cave. Swimming in the light makes the water glisten and change into silver, gold, green, and turquoise. We enjoy a swim in the cave, then putt-putt along the south coast of the island comparing our college knowledge of geology to try to explain the unusual rock formations and coves.

READY TO JUMP OUTSIDE THE GREEN CAVE

Our son-in-law, Tom and our grandchildren, as well as a lot of tourists, have found the roof of the cave and the high banks just outside to be their favorite place to jump straight down 20 feet into the clear deep sea. I do a lot of praying during this activity.

Our next destination is Stiniva, a cove that is pictured on a poster on our dining room wall. We squeeze between sheer high cliffs on both sides into a small inlet about one boat-width wide with a wonderful white marble-like stone beach and the usual clear turquoise water. While we snorkel around, we find an area in the shade where the underwater plants on the rocks are a beautiful lavender color. There are several sailboats anchored outside and people swimming back and forth. As part of the interesting scenery, we watch a heavy set diver climb into his small boat, change from his wet suit to his birthday suit, and give us a "full moon" view as he leans over to do something in his boat.

We can't ask Drago to always provide the boat, so we find and buy a small outboard motor boat. It works for a year or so, but it can only take four people and there are usually lots more who want a boat ride. *No matter what size boat a guy has, he always wants one a little bigger.*

John has engineered a skid/winch system to bring the boat out of the water onto our rocky shore. This is a necessity, as the weather is not totally predictable and even if it was, we may not hear or understand the *"prognosis"*. John, Drago and I experiment with methods to get the boat up and down the ramp. We spend most of a day down on the beach putting in rollers on the ramp for the boat. We can now bring it up and down by ourselves. John brags that it only takes five minutes to put the boat in the sea. *I know it takes most of an hour to get everything down to the sea, the battery installed, the boat into the sea and ready to go, but that's okay....... We plan for five minutes and wait.*

Next, John purchases a used 4.6 meter fiberglass "pasera", the most typical small boat on Vis, which was actually built in Komiža. It is a little longer, much heavier, and quite a bit higher on the sides than our previous boat. It has a hand cranked "put- put" diesel engine like the one in Drago's boat, but we carry an electric motor on the back just in case. The seller tells us the engine is a gift; that it is not part of the price, and needs some work; it doesn't have neutral or reverse gears.

Dinko and John take the boat out to Ravnik. John leaves Dinko to fish on the island while he fine tunes the GPS and fish finder, discovering that he had put the transponder together wrong and it was measuring sideways. *Can you believe that he admitted this?* Dinko catches a mess of fine quality fish, and puts some of it on our grill for dinner when they come in. This is my kind of fishing. This boat is definitely an improvement over the small one.

They had considerable difficulty getting Dinko in and out of the boat at Ravnik, mostly because he couldn't reverse the boat. With this in mind, John "invents" and builds from stainless steel, an apparatus to replace the rudder on our boat to change the direction of the water to let the boat go in reverse using the same principle as a jet boat. We take the boat on Drago's makeshift trailer over to Rukavac to launch it and see how the new rudder works. It works just about as planned, but at a little slower speed than we thought it would. Nevertheless, it immediately stops the boat from going forward, so docking near rocks should be much safer. We pull the boat out again

189

and bring it home to get ready to put in a new motor with a reverse gear. *What? What was the purpose of this rudder if you put in a new motor and transmission with reverse? He just has to see if these things will work.*

****

Anyone who owns a boat of any size knows that a good deal of time and money goes into maintenance and repairs. These rocks can be sharp and somehow we have a small hole in the hull. We need to make a fiberglass repair on our boat. We are told to go to a store in Komiža to get the fiberglass. About the size of a bathroom, this little store carries everything from fishing tackle, swim suits, shoes, boat supplies, to hardware. They usually have what we need. John tries his Croatian and looks up words in our ever present Croatian dictionary to ask for the fiberglass, but the lady says, "No, we don't have this". *It is time to try in English.* After some discussion she decides she does have the fiberglass, but she can't sell it today because she will close the store in 15 minutes. He will have to come back tomorrow with his own containers because the two components of the resin are in bulk barrels. We find an almost empty water bottle on a table, ask a guy nearby if we could have it and take it back to get it filled. Now we need a small bottle for the other component, so John goes to a nearby coffee bar and brings back a juice bottle. Since the proprietor is alone in the store, we wait until she is closed, then follow her up a narrow passageway to her warehouse which is the size of a small bedroom. She transfers the two components into our bottles and we get 2 square meters of fiberglass cloth for about $6.

****

CHAPTER 28

MEMORABLE MOMENTS

Cousin Joško silently organizes many of the special cultural events for tourism on the island. As part of his duties as chairman of the organization to keep Vis traditions alive, he has organized two concerts by Filip Devic, a well known Klapa group from Split. He asks us if we will host the group between concerts. We are anxious to be a part of the tradition and Croatian Klapa harmony is my new favorite music so we jump at the chance.

The first concert is to be held in the *Zelena Spelija* (The Green Cave) on the backside of Ravnik Island which is only accessible by boat. On the evening of the concert, the sea is *bonaca* (calm and flat) so the concert in the Green Cave will be held. Just before dark, with cousins, Maja and Liljana, and her 6 year-old grandson, Stipe, filling our first little boat to capacity, we motor around the corner to the village of Rukavac to join the flotilla to the cave.

At the proper time a bonfire on the island signals for the flotilla to begin. The Klapa singers, dressed in black trousers, white shirts and red cummerbunds board the replica Falkuža fishing boat. The sail has been dismantled to allow the boat to enter the cave. The five-man crew, dressed in Dalmatian navy and white striped t-shirts stand to push and pull the giant oars. As they begin the short journey, they all begin to sing, Visu Moj, the official Vis Hymn. *WOW. I have never experienced anything like this.*

At night, the cave has a completely different atmosphere. As we quietly row into the cave, ropes are extended from one boat to the next. Rubber bumpers hang down to absorb the bumping together. Slow swells enter the cave causing the thirty or so boats to bob slowly up and down. The sea laps against the sides of the cave and the boats. One light bulb, powered by a battery, hangs down from the hole in the ceiling. The rising full moon pours its shimmery light through the two entrances to illuminate the scene. Even the bats, non-existent during our day swims, must wonder what has happened to their homes. They stop their shrill squeaking and darting around to listen to the music in this acoustically perfect setting.

I am sitting in the bow of our tiny boat, totally enthralled with the concert when I feel my feet getting wet. I look down to see that we are taking in water. *What if our boat sank in the middle of the concert? How embarrassing would that be?* I find a little plastic can in the bottom of the boat and proceed to bail out the water....trying to be very quiet and invisible, because even pouring water will disturb the ambiance. With each cupful I bend down and scoop up a little water, then twist around to toss it quietly over the side.

On the way back we watch as a speedboat full of Slovenians heads back to Rukavac....in reverse, which they say is the only choice at this moment. They refuse a tow from a larger boat, and continue their backwards trip. *A comical end to a beautiful evening.*

The next morning, Drago, Rina and her cousin, Inis from Zagreb, arrive at 8 am with everything we need for our Klapa picnic. The ladies, including Liljana and Maja who stayed over night, clean every corner, bathroom and window of the house and terrace. Inis gives me a very professional massage to relax my back, which has developed a painful *kitchma* from bailing the boat. Joško and Vedrana bring a carload of grape prunings for the grill, a 5 liter jug of his red Plavac wine and a 5 liter jug of his white Vugava wine. Inis and Rina prepare chicken shish kebobs and marinated pork chops for the grill. Drago prepares and mans the grill. Inis and Maja put together a wonderful pasta salad. I make a very American potato salad without celery. *Why without celery? There is none to be found on this island...only celery root with some small bitter stems.*

The Klapa group and their wives arrive around 11 am. They are well-educated, interesting people who speak good English. They all have other occupations and practice together two or three times a week. They do it because they love to sing and they want to keep the Croatian Klapa tradition alive. Bravo! The weather and the sea are perfect. All the guests have a swim before the meal. John takes a boatload out to experience the Green Cave in the daytime.

I love this method of entertaining. John and I visit with the guests and everyone else cooks, serves and cleans up. The Repanić family is as anxious as we are to be a part of this. After dinner, the singers bring out a mandolin and a guitar and entertain us for more than an hour with wonderful Croatian folk songs. They are still in their swim trunks and flip-flops, sitting around casually, drinking wine and singing in wonderful harmony. Everyone else knows the words and a harmony part to sing. I have no idea about the words, but somehow it is easy to sing along. Although my back is telling me not to, I have a dance with Srđan, one of the organizers who just last week was the telephone repairman who came to our house. They tell us, "This is how we love to sing; no stress and lots of fun and laughter." John asks, "Do Klapa groups ever sing the national anthem?" "Oh yes" is the immediate answer. They all stand up, put on their shirts and shoes, slick their hair and look for a flag. Our decorative American flag windsock with a Croatian flag pinned onto one side will do. They move it so they can all stand under it and belt out a serious, beautiful rendition of the Croatian National Anthem. They know the tune and we know the words of the Star Spangled Banner. Together, we attempt to sing it. We had invited the neighbors to come over, but they all listen from their terraces.

The party moves down to the sea. Swimming in the Adriatic Sea is a social event. Because it takes no effort to stay afloat, people float around gossiping and chatting. This group sings a song about the sea and on cue they all go under water at the same time.

Our guest book is a mural of the sea on our stairway walls. I provide paints and brushes. Our guests add to the sea scene. We have everything from a multicolored snail done by a five year old, to a mermaid painted by a professional. Some guests get right into adding something and others choose not to. I tell them, anything goes. One of the Filip Devic singers draws a large fish that they all sign. *Memorable.*

As they leave, they express to us that this should be an annual event. We agree. The next year when I see some of them at the concert, they tell me they are looking forward to that great potato salad again. I haven't planned on it, but put it together before the party. *Without celery.*

That evening we attend the concert in the outdoor courtyard of the Baterijia, an old fortress that now houses the Vis museum.

****

Joško leads us up the hill from Dračevo Polje to Tališ, the site of a major Illyrian (pre-Greek) city from the 3rd and 4th century BC. Illyrian coins found on the island and elsewhere have Tališ written on them. We drive through the small village of Duboka and up a steep rocky road in 4 wheel drive, low range. We walk through a very narrow long military tunnel which comes out onto the top of the hill with walls painted with camouflage. This is one of many Yugoslav army installations from the cold war era. After WW II this area was a fairly extensive military defense complex with numerous tunnels and bunkers and artillery sites. It has been returned from the military to civilian use which is typical of many parts of the island. On one hill is a large "pyramid" (an extra large rock pile) where the Illyrian king is supposedly buried. There is a very old villa which is being restored for tourist apartments. The view from here is spectacular down into the valley and out to the sea. These tunnels are clean and safe and our grandsons love to explore them.

JOHN, NATHAN, ALEX, MONICA AND LORI
EXPLORING THE MILITARY TUNNELS

While Drago's boyhood friend, Ljudva, was working on the garage roof, we had invited him to bring his wife, Maria, to stay in our apartment for a vacation in August. They live in northern Croatia on a small farm, far from the sea. They speak NO English. At this point our Croatian is minimal. This will be their first ever vacation.

They travel all day by bus to Split and arrive around 11 pm on the fast passenger ferry with a large ice chest full of homegrown meat, sausages, prsut (prosciutto), and wine. They are coming for a vacation, but Ljudva told Drago that Maria would do all the cooking for them and us, and he will do some work around. Maybe she doesn't trust the American to cook for them.

Ljudva starts his day with a glass of homemade slivovica, a very strong prune brandy, and black thick coffee. Maria starts her vacation by cleaning all my floors with a damp rag. *I thought they were already clean.* Around 9:30 am, they have breakfast of bread and sausages, and then start to prepare dinner. For the required thin soup first course, I watch Maria boil a chicken, then remove it from the broth. Ljudva informs me that every day he must eat something with a spoon (soup). When I return from a swim, Ljudva and Maria are sitting at the table eating the chicken. It apparently is not going to be part of the meal, but a snack. Fifteen minutes later, at lunch we eat the broth with no chicken in it, and ribs and potatoes. Each day is something new for our 2 pm dinners; Pork goulash over macaroni, baked chicken with tons of potatoes, grilled pork ribs, all prepared with globs of lard, which make everything taste delicious. *Never mind those calories and cholesterol.* There is always a warm, sweet irresistible kolach with poppy seeds or ground walnuts for desert.

The oven and cook top are on full heat all morning. The hot sun beats in. Maria and Ljudva don't seem to mind the heat. I turn on our ceiling fans and open the doors and windows to cool the house. When I return from another swim, they have closed things down again. They don't like moving air. *Okay, they are cooking...they win.*

We eat outside on the terrace for two hours. These are not large people and seem to be able to metabolize all these calories. *If I stayed on this Northern Croatian diet any longer, I would be huge.* This is very different from the Dalmatian diet of olive oil, fish and vegetables or my normal summer meal of a cool salad, thrown together just before meal time. *Minimum cooking is my mantra in the hot weather.*

Ljudva and John put wall tile around the mini kitchen in the apartment. Maria is a cleaning machine. She moves furniture, and bends at the hips to clean the floors. *How can she do that after eating a huge meal? My windows and floors are shining...all the time. She won't let me near the kitchen to do the dishes. I stay out of the way down at the beach. Whose vacation is this?*

We take them in the boat to the Green Cave and sightseeing in the car. One evening we all go into Vis for the *"Viski Noč"* festival, complete with grilled sardines on the Riva, and a concert in the square. They spend an hour near the sea each day. Maria doesn't swim, but wades just up to her knees. They are very happy with their first "vacation". After a week, she is very homesick for her baby grandson and her mother, who live with them in their four generation home.

We drive Ljudva and Maria back to Lepoglava because Ivan has our European headlights and tires for the Jeep ready to install. Maria is ecstatic to be home in her own kitchen with her darling little grandson. We sleep overnight in their large home which Ljudva and Maria built by themselves. Beautiful, detailed woodwork shows off Ljudva's talents. Well kept chickens, pigs, rabbits, and ducks and a large bountiful garden, help us understand why they wanted to bring their own food. Nearby, and up the steep hill, he proudly shows us his vineyards and his small farmhouse where he produces his own wine in the konoba. *We feel so lucky to have the chance to get to know these folks who are truly the salt of the earth.*

****

The Brits have found Vis to be a great alternative to other over-developed and over-priced Mediterranean areas, and are purchasing the old stone homes to renovate for holiday homes. On one of our first encounters, John meets a family from London at the tennis court and invites them out to our villa for lunch, a swim and trip out to the Green Cave. We enjoy a great afternoon with Tony and Lucinda and their two young children, George and Teddy.

Late in the afternoon, the local hotel owner, Božen, calls to request the pleasure of our company at a get-together for the Croatian/English granddaughter of Ivan Mestrović, the famous Croatian sculptor. She and her husband are purchasing property on the island. The details are a little sketchy, but we know the affair is to be at Božen's newly acquired property at Dračevo Polje, and we are all to meet at the hotel at 7:30 to caravan out to the party. We take Tony and Lucinda and the children into Vis so they have time to prepare for the party, then hurry back to our place to shower and dress in time to arrive at 7:30. We are asked to wait outside the hotel, as the guest of honor is still napping and will be an hour late. We wait around talking to some of the youngest Repanić relatives that happen to be playing around the hotel.

Finally, it is time to caravan out to Dračevo Polje for the dinner/reception/event. The hotel car is loaded with appetizers. Božen delegates Tony to drive this car to the dinner. *Never mind that he is from London... normally drives on the "wrong side" and has not driven on the narrow, windy roads that have no shoulder, but have four foot drop-offs on both sides.* There is no room in that car for George and Teddy, so they climb in the backseat of our car. We follow the pre-arranged instructions to follow the caravan from the parking lot. After waiting for about 20 minutes in the parking lot for the "caravan" to go past, John walks to the hotel and learns that they just left on a different route out of town. We start out. We know how to get to Dračevo Polje. The children are confident that they have been to the right place and they will know it when we see it, but their memories are not very accurate in the dark. We drive past a few times, looking for a clue. Finally, Lucinda walks down to the main road to find her children that she has sent with these strangers. She admits that in London, she never lets the children out of her sight, except when they are in school. The children were delightful, asking all kinds of questions about America. Lucinda reports that Tony drove off the side of the road, ran over something, and had two flat tires. They left the car along the road, and transferred everything to another car.

We find a glass of wine, and visit for a few minutes with Ivana, the guest of honor, who is not particularly interested in us, and her husband, Anthony. By now, it is too dark to see anything. The only light is flickering from a few candles placed in the dry weeds and the occasional small fires that flare up and are stomped out. At 9:25, someone announces that the taxi is here to take the group to Darko's restaurant for dinner. The group of about ten English investors departs. Božen thanks us for coming and we are left with Tony's family, Božen and his nine year old daughter, and the family that had sold this property to Božen. There are a few slices of bread, a dollop of fish pate and a few slices of cheese left on the appetizer plates. *That is dinner. This event is not the result of bad manners, but an example of what happens when both parties have limited knowledge of each other's language. It is just poor communication.*

****

Just before grape harvest, the Sabatina festival is celebrated in the village of Podspelia. When we arrive with my brother Bob and his wife Diane, around 7 pm, we are encouraged to help ourselves to the local wine from large basket-covered bottles. The village men are carefully loading and turning sardines on the hot grills with their fingers. Hot! Rina shows us the drill. We take a thick slice of bread from a basket, and then wait in line to have some hot sardines placed on the bread. There are no tables so we eat standing up. We have tried this before. It is tricky to get out the bones and head, without dropping the whole thing, but we manage and they are delicious and free.

When we have had our fill of sardines, we follow the crowd into the village cultural hall, up well-worn stairs to the second floor auditorium and sit at an inconspicuous table to watch the festivities. Local women bring wine and beautiful bunches of grapes to our table. No charge. Everyone stands while the priest blesses the harvest and the crop and apparently cracks a few jokes that we don't understand. In a skit, the village women, one by one, come down between tables balancing baskets of grapes on their heads. They present their grapes to a tester who gives them approval or disapproval. Rina is the last one. She swaggers to the table, looking for all the world like a peasant woman. When she approaches the table there is considerable heated discussion with the tester, and lots of laughter from the audience. She is a talented actress.

A local Klapa group sings a few songs with the audience singing along. We are enjoying the music when we hear a crash. One man picks himself up off the floor. The legs of his old plastic chair had slowly started spreading apart until one of the legs snapped. Within an hour, at least five more chairs collapse. Now people are scrambling to stack two chairs together to avoid the embarrassment of crashing to the floor. The next time we went to an event at the Podspelia hall, they had all new chairs. *What fun is that?*

When the band starts playing, we don't recognize any of the songs, but everyone is singing along, dancing, and having a great time. Each piece lasts about 20 minutes and picks up speed as it goes. No one gives up. These folks actually dance WITH each other…touching.

Unfortunately, they are also filling the air with cigarette smoke and we finally leave so we can breathe. And here is the greatest inconsistency on this island, Croatia and even in Europe. Vis has air as clean as it can get and the Vis folks claim it as such and are proud of their clean, unpolluted environment. They use almost no pesticides or herbicides, love the ecological food, etc, yet a high percentage smoke cigarettes. Thank goodness recent laws have been passed to prohibit smoking in public places and restaurants. The price of cigarettes is exorbitant for their small incomes. They have put death warnings on the packages and yet they smoke. *Go figure!*

****

One day our breakfast on the terrace is enhanced by peering through binoculars and the telescope watching seven guys come in by boat to the island of Ravnik, across from us, to herd the small band of resident sheep. We have always wondered how they get these sheep onto and off of the island. *It is a trick just to get people out of boats onto the rocks …but sheep?* The guys walked through the really scratchy brush (we've never found any good trails) with the thousands of nesting seagulls squawking and dive bombing to protest the intrusion. One guy even had on shorts. *Ouch.* They somehow gathered all the sheep and walked them along the rocky shore until they came to a small stone enclosure. We have wondered about its use. They held the sheep there for a couple of hours, and then set them all free …minus their wool. It must be sheep shearing time. *I guess we will have to wait to see how they get them into boats.*

****

JOŠKO, MOTHER MARE, RINA AND DINKO

JERINA, ME (PAT), JOHN AND JOŠKO (JOZO)

CHAPTER 29

THE VIS FAMILY TODAY

These "cousins", who are actually John's second cousins, have been wonderful friends. They are all as different from each other as people can be.

Jerina seems to be everyone's friend and has been a delight from the beginning. Her infectious laugh sparks the family gatherings. We have always been able to understand each other by charades and body language. She has never married and lives on her small pension, in a few rooms of her large 300 year old house on the street behind the Riva. She spent her working years as a secretary for the government owned winery.

For the first few years that we were on Vis she was tied to her home, caretaking her mother, Perina. When Perina died, Jerina had the opportunity to venture out. When we offered to take her to Rijeka to visit her brother, Jozo, she said she could go, but only if we went by overnight ferry, so we took her with our car on the Jadrolinija overnight ferry from Split. John and I found a place to sleep, not comfortably, but we did manage a few winks. Jerina sat in the same place for the whole voyage and never even closed her eyes. After a great visit with her family she decided it would be okay to drive back to Split in the car. We have made a few successful car trips since then. She seldom goes to Split, maintaining that everything she needs is here in Vis. *And probably it is.*

Jerina's brother, Joško, (Jozo) and his Rijeka family have been superb hosts to us when we visit Rijeka. Jozo, a retired city bus driver for Rijeka, passed away last year and we miss his smile and friendship. Son, Tonchi, a sea captain, and his wife Loreta, a bank credit manager, have built a beautiful new home overlooking Opatija. The youngest son, Altiero, married a Texas girl, Joan. They live in Austin and they visit every year in Croatia. It has been a delight to watch Jozo's talented granddaughters grow up. At a very young age, Ivana could translate between Croatian, English and Italian and play the piano like a maestro. Younger sister Josipa keeps us amused with her great sense of humor and charm.

When we first came to Vis the other Joško and his wife, Vedrana, lived at Dračevo Polje in the little stone house. They had just retired from their jobs in Split and were happy caring for their vineyards. After the family divided the land, they reluctantly moved into the Vis apartment of his mother, Mare. They moved her into the old folks home where she didn't have to deal with three rickety flights of stairs, and brother Dinko moved into the Dračevo Polje house. They still care for their vineyards and olives, and make wine, but it is all done from the even smaller original Repanić house where he was born, now just a wine cellar. He sings bass and is the organizer of the local Klapa singers, and the mover-shaker for maintaining the traditions and festivals of the people from the fields.

Their only son, Siniša works at the same job in the Split shipyard that Joško worked at until his retirement. His wife Elza is an elementary school teacher. They live in the same Split apartment that Joško and Vedrana lived in.We have enjoyed watching this family grow. Their two boys ten years ago were the shyest I had ever seen. Now Pino is a tall, good-looking, friendly university student studying history. Marino is a very friendly outgoing teenager.

Ten years ago, Dinko was working for the hotel and living in Komiža with his wife Sonja and his grandaughter, Sandra. Their coffee bar had to close because they didn't have toilet facilities in the space they rented. They had always used the facilities in the tiny grocery store next door, which closed at the same time the larger grocery store opened near Vis town. The tiny grocery store has been replaced by a fishing supply store, that won't share the toilet. The landlord's brother opened a coffee bar next door, and didn't want the competition. *Free enterprise at work.*

When Dinko retired he moved out to the little stone house in Dračevo Polje, but Sonja continued to live in Komiža. They have separated and Dinko lives by himself on his small pension and cares for his vines and olive trees. For ten years there has been a hope in Dračevo Polje that they will get city water piped to their homes. It hasn't happened yet. He plays bocce on several teams and sings bass in the Komiža Klapa group. He is always looking for a new lady to share his life.

When Sandra was 14 years old she translated for my interview with her great grandmother Mare. When we arrived at Mare's apartment she was reading her Catholic prayer book and saying her rosary. She told me she would be 90 next month and wonders why she is still alive. Her heart is in the vineyard at Dračevo Polje and she is very sad that she cannot work, or walk very well. She said her mind is not good. The fact that her two sons don't get along together bothers her. She feels it is her fault but doesn't know how to resolve the problems. She said she had been like dead until I came today, and now she feels alive again and maybe life is okay. Maybe her purpose in life now is to tell the stories of her life. She was extremely animated; laughing, crying, getting out of her chair to demonstrate dancing and working in the vineyards. I was afraid we would tire Mare out, but when I suggested we leave, she insisted she could talk all day about her life. She took a well worn envelope from her purse and proudly showed me a few pictures of her grandchildren as children thirty years ago. A couple of times Mare came to tears as she related her very difficult life.

Sandra had no idea how difficult her great grandmother's life had been and came away with an appreciation of how easy she has it. She said she would never complain about walking to the beach again. Her schedule at the small high school in Vis for EVERY DAY included 14 classes: Italian, Latin, English, Croatian grammar, Croatian history, world history, music, art, math, physics, biology, chemistry, and geography and computer. They have a short lecture, an assignment and are expected to do most of their work out of class. Sandra is also a talented dancer and musician. She graduated from the high school on Vis, did extremely well on the entrance exams for the university, and attended the University in Split. Her Serbian father, who was not part of her life up until she was 18 years old, has come around and is helping her with university costs and has taken her to his home in Australia for visits with his family.

Rina continues to amaze us with her dramatic readings which are a big part of every festival and concert. When we drop in on Rina she fixes a plate of bread, salami and cheese, and offers us wine. She starts telling us the story of her life. We are fascinated and struggling to understand all the Croatian. In her usual dramatic way, she tells us of her life as a young woman wanting desperately to go to art school. That was not possible because of lack of money, so she spent some time in agricultural school with a stipend before dropping out to find work for a short time in a restaurant in Split. She spent more than 30

203

years working on the island in the uniform factory ironing all day with heavy irons. Being on time was always her problem....and it still is.

Now on a small pension she gets out to the field as often as possible to gather wild asparagus, mushrooms, greens, capers or whatever it is at the moment.

Our decision to gamble on Drago to work on the house has been a phenomenal experience. As honest as a man can be, he is everyone's friend, and yet knows all the angles of how to get things done with the bureaucracy. He knows how to build anything made of concrete or stone and is the handyman for Vis. He has built a house for himself and Rina on the hill above Vis with the most imagination and least cost. He is a master scavenger of building materials. Drago and Rina's son, Stipe lives with them and works in the summer for the city ushering in tourist yachts to the harbor. A talented artist and musician, he is always searching for his next project.

Liljana and Maja, the cousins from Petar's line, have become our great friends. When they are on the island we spend many fun hours together. Liljana, after retiring as the head nurse in a pediatric ward of the hospital in Split, gives many volunteer hours to the diabetic association. Maja continues to teach her kindergarten classes in Serbia.

We have experienced birthdays, births, deaths and family celebrations, arguments, and tragedies. The older generation, Mare, Perina and Dobrila have all passed away. We feel so lucky to have known them for a few years.

The family claims that we have been a catalyst for getting the family together. Without us here, they say they would seldom get together, and their family feuds would probably be more intense.

JOŠKO, DRAGO AND SINIŠA

MARE WITH OUR DAUGHTER, LORI

VEDRANA, MARE, RINA, JERINA, MAJA, DINKO,
LILJANA AND JOSKO SINGING TOGETHER

JERINA, MAJA AND LILJANA

CHAPTER 30

WHERE WE ARE IN 2011?

How have our justifications for buying the property on Vis turned out?

"Life here is like returning to small town America in the 1950's and 1960's which suits us just fine".

When we walk along the Riva in Vis to go to the bank or post office, it always takes longer than expected because there are always friends, acquaintances, relatives, or someone to greet with "dobar dan" and ask how they and their family are doing. The vegetable vendors steer us to the freshest produce they have to offer. The lady in the bread store knows that I want *bakin krug* (unsliced whole wheat) and she will save it for me if I call ahead. The three gals who work in the bank ask about our family and we ask about theirs. Children play unsupervised along the Riva with no barriers to the sea. Everyone is watching out for them.

There are only white, clean, usually nicely dressed folks here. The several catholic churches are well attended. We see no radical, punk type young people and very few overweight people. Many smoke too much, but are learning to be considerate of non-smokers with the new laws forbidding smoking in public buildings, most restaurants and inside the ferry. Although they drink a lot of wine (usually diluted with water), some beer and enjoy their flavored brandy aperitifs, we have never seen anyone intoxicated.

It is customary for the wife to join the husband's family when they marry, often moving in with them. They normally only have one or two children and it seems to me that the first child often is on its way when they marry. The husband may be the main family decision maker, but the women seem to have major input into family life. Both parents care for the children, but the women take care of the elderly parents. Many women work outside the home and grandmothers are the main babysitters. Many of the men are seamen and may be gone for several months at a time.

Family incomes here range from $500 to $1000 a month. The government statistics say it takes $700 to $900 a month to live. Only 9% have more than they need to live and 11% have just enough to live. *It is a lot easier to live here with American retirement than on their small pensions.* My observation is that everyone eats well from fishing, vegetable gardens and a great barter system. No one is homeless, although they may share a very small space with lots of family. Material possessions are unimportant, except for nice clothes. Everyone owns a mobile phone…but the cheapest they can find. Most of our neighbors own an apartment in Split or Zagreb, and their weekend house on Vis. Most own some land with a small vineyard or olive grove. Very little of the land is in the plan for building, so it is of low value to sell unless it has some remnant of a house on it.

Keeping the island natural and eating natural foods is very important to them. Some tell us that life during the communist era of the 60's and 70's was easier. Everyone had a job, maybe with nothing to do. The government provided a house. The problem was that there was little production and the economy was not sustained. When Tito died in 1980, life became less tolerable. They wish their economy would improve more quickly and they still don't trust their politicians.

What's new?

As we listen to the news of snipers, kidnapers and terrorists in America and the rest of the world, we have asked people here about crime on the island, knowing that we miss a lot because we don't understand everything in their language. Crime on the island is minor, especially since the get-away has to be by ferry that only leaves Vis twice a day. Although they talk about mafia, that is usually referring to politicians or people selling merchandise on the black market, charging too much for something or owning more than the average person.

Our Bargujac neighborhood is bustling in the summer with returning families who own the weekend houses. Most of our neighbors have the same last name, Vojković, and so they are related one way or the other. I haven't sorted out all these relationships. They are well educated and have retired from jobs as engineers, teachers, musicians, translators, etc. Now fishing is the passion of the men.

VOJKO VOJKOVIĆ MENDING HIS FISH NETS AT
BARGUJAC MARINA

Our next door neighbor, Tonka, a very gracious, gentle lady comes from Split whenever possible in the spring, summer and fall. The house belongs to her deceased husband's daughter, but Tonka takes special care of the flowers and the house. Her description of the early life in Bargujac is amazing:

When she and her husband built their weekend house about 30 years ago there was no road, so she and her husband hauled stones, blocks and cement in by wheelbarrow about a half mile on a trail. Because there was no electricity or water they mixed their concrete by hand in buckets and used sea water. The gravel came in their boats from Budikovac, a nearby island.

Winter is a different story. Three or four retired couples, including us, enjoy the solitude of Bargujac. The men spend their time mending their fish nets or fishing whenever the weather will allow. They can't believe that we want to work on our house or keep so active.

We don't get involved with the local gossip mostly because of the language thing, so we naively think everyone and everything is good. We hear that brothers with houses next to each other don't speak to each other. We have no idea why. Everyone seems friendly to us. People wave as we pass in the car. That may be because on most of the roads we must slow down and pull over to pass each other. There is only one road where we can drive over 40 miles per hour.

Life goes on at a slow pace.....*polako* is the mantra for Vis. Most stores are open in the morning, then close from noon until around 5 pm when they open for the evening. Summer time Vis is swarming with tourists who are mostly staying in private apartments. Winter is quiet with many retired folks and virtually no tourists.

A dream world…maybe. But with today's amazing technology we are connected by satellite television to the world. The internet provides Skype at a very low or no cost, and now with a special phone, we don't even need the computer on. Most of our USA business can be done online and we have our USA mail delivered immediately by a virtual mail service. We can have it scanned, download it and print it or have it mailed to anywhere or trash it. Google easily translates any Croatian documents into not quite perfect English for us. What more do we need?

"We like everything about this island."

We love the Mediterranean climate. The residents complain before the temperature gets close to the maximum of 90 degrees F with "*vruć je*" (it's really hot), and when it falls below 40 degrees F it is "*zima je*" (it's really cold). A *jugo* south wind brings on the headaches, bad tempers, etc. and everything gets blamed on the *jugo*. They really don't seem to appreciate the mild climate and the absence of hurricanes, tornadoes, floods, blizzards and all those things that the rest of the world deals with.

We love the music and that the Vis people love to sing, are very good at it and like to perform. As I listen to an evening concert of the island Klapa groups, I feel as if I could be in Carnegie Hall and can't believe that this quality of harmony is being performed in the Hrvatska Dom upstairs over a restaurant with a just a handful people in the audience. Music is multi-generational with the young and very old all participating together. We love that Croatian television broadcasts many concerts live, in their entirety, with no commercials.

210

We thoroughly enjoy the year round colorful wild flowers, the simple food, and the friendly people. My great pleasure is swimming, exercising and snorkeling in the warm clean, turquoise clear sea. John, like most Vis men, only enjoys being in the sea when it is really, really warm. I never tire of admiring the always changing sky, and taking in the smells, and the fresh air. We both love delving into the mysteries of the rock piles, and the ancient and modern history.

Part of the enjoyment of the tourist season is watching the endless parade of tourist yachts and sailboats, both charter and private. Many of them stop overnight in our view to avoid the busy harbors and marinas. They haul out their big water toys and just have fun.

We are ardent fans of the island festivals and concerts. We are still discovering new things and we say that when we don't ooh and ahh over the view coming over the hill into Vis town it will be time to leave.

"There is so much to learn here and so many stories to tell."

Boris, the archeologist and director of the super Vis museum asks us to meet him to see his newest finds. *AMAZING!* He and his small crew have unearthed the remains of two Greek houses, from 2 centuries BC. They are in the old town of Issa, above the hotel in Vis, buried in one of the small fields between the rock terraces. He shows us what was Greek (the dry construction) and what was added by the Romans with mortar, centuries later. He was very excited about his discovery of eighty four Roman coins in one corner under a stone and the print of a skin bag.

Between the two houses are stone roads with a drainage area between them. Beside one of the houses is the base of the original town wall with huge slabs of rock two meters wide at the bottom. This is the first real finding of actual buildings in Issa. Boris's knowledge is amazing. He can tell from the color of the soil, what happened in each part. He found the remains of a pot with salted sardines in one corner. The cleaned pieces of pottery and tools are in a small tin building without a lock......maybe under occasional police patrol.

The natives have taught us so many important health tips. I think there must have been a national effort to educate the people that:

1. You never stay in a wet swim suit because it will damage your female parts. You always take an extra suit to the beach. The women know a trick I have yet to master, which is changing inside a towel from the wet suit to the dry one without showing a thing. A bikini is a must as this process is totally impossible in a one piece suit. Or, you can just lie in the sun, al fresco and not worry about that wet suit.

2. You never go in the strong sun between 10 in the morning and 4 in the afternoon.

3. It is really bad to sit on a cold stone or concrete, especially for women as it will damage your female parts.

4. If you sweat, you need to change immediately to dry clothes as a damp shirt will give you a cold for sure. You certainly can't sit in a breeze if you have been sweating.

5. Everyday you should eat something with a spoon. (soup) . On the other hand, in winter, don't drink anything from the refrigerator and for sure no ice (the ice thing goes for summer too.)

6. Moving air in a house or car will give you liver (or kidney) problems.

I think these are all good ideas and I have been reprimanded more than once for crossing those lines, but, why haven't they figured out that smoking kills?

"It will be a beautiful place for our family and friends to visit."

We've talked with a lot of grandparents who agree that visiting teenage grandchildren in their own homes is kind of like becoming a piece of furniture. The kids are more interested in their friends, their video games, their sports, etc. than they are in Grandma and Grandpa. BUT, when our grandchildren come to Vis, they are in a new realm.

They spend most of the day snorkeling and swimming or absorbing the sunshine (sometimes between 10 and 4 and always with sunscreen). We take them on adventures not possible in the USA. We explore abandoned military tunnels. They jump off cliffs into the clear, deep sea. We hike to caves to see the stalactites and stalagmites, eat in interesting restaurants, and visit in homes completely different from what they know in the USA. They have opportunities to meet kids from different cultures, who like to practice their English. They love it and we can actually talk to them here. Yes, they bring their addictive electronic devices and we wish they would leave them home, but the quality time we spend with them here is just not possible when we are in their domain. Our oldest grandson, Alex has completed 2 years of university level Croatian language in the USA and has a Croatian flag hanging in his dorm room. Vis has made an impression on him.

GRANDAUGHTERS JILL AND AMY ON HILL HUM
OVERLOOKING KOMIŽA

CROATIAN AND AMERICAN COUSINS GET TO KNOW
EACH OTHER

GRANDKIDS MONICA AND ALEX WITH THEIR OCTOPUS
CATCH

One of the greatest advantages of being abroad is that many of our "old" friends and siblings, cousins, etc. have spent several weeks here visiting, relaxing and exploring. Sometimes it is an add-on to their planned European vacation and sometimes we explore Europe together.

Our adventures with them could be another book, but I know stories about other people's traveling aren't that interesting. It is such a pleasure to spend time with these folks, getting to know them better, and showing them whatever interests them on the island. We know we would not have spent as much time with any of them in the USA.

Part of the charm and interest here is the many new friends we have made from all over the world. They are here for short times to enjoy their "holiday houses" or just short term tourists that we show around the island. We have wonderful conversations and have a great time comparing and joking about our different cultures.

"This is a great place to use as a base for traveling in Europe."

We load up our nine passenger van with grandkids and sometimes their friends, daughter Lori and camping gear. Lori plans the trip and navigates, John drives and I enjoy the kids in the back seat. The campgrounds in Europe are super. They are easy to find, cheap, clean and always have space for a tent and a car no matter what time you get in. The kids sleep in the tent and we make up a bed in the van.

Together we have seen World War II museums and battlefields in France, Belgium and Netherlands. We have crossed the English Channel and explored England for a family wedding. Together we have toured Germany, Austria, London, Paris including Disneyland, Rome, Pompeii, Pisa, Bosnia and Herzegovina, and Serbia. They have seen most of Croatia.

With friends, we have driven to the Czech Republic, Poland, Hungary, Germany, England, France, Slovakia, Austria, Italy, Greece and all points in between, including Albania. It is a super way to tour and this has been a perfect base for our traveling. We have so many memories and about 10,000 pictures. We still have places to see.

"Maybe it will be a good investment."

What we now call our "villa" has been a terrific investment. Croatia has decreed that there will be no more building within 150 meters of the sea. We are in a protected green zone in one of the most beautiful parts of the world. There can be no more houses built near us and our property value has increased ten fold. Lori tells us we can never sell because she loves the place so much. Time and circumstances will tell.

"John will always have a project to keep him busy and challenged."

Eleven years ago, when we bought our property on Vis, our plan was to be on Vis a few months a year, and live in the USA for our retired years. We tried full-time RVing.....not for us. We planned and got permits to build a house in California. John had enjoyed building our three farm houses and he wanted to do much of the new building himself to keep himself (and me) in good condition. As we started the process we decided that the California bureaucracy was more than we wanted to deal with.

We looked at the possibilities of building on Vis. The moratorium that has been in effect since 2005 was a prohibitive problem (and still is) for any new building, but we had a permit to finish our existing house without a deadline or plan.

So we are on Vis most of the year, improving our own house on our own schedule and on our own terms. We have added a garage with an apartment above, a shade cover for our front terrace, a swimming pool for those days the sea is not good for swimming, a couple more guest bedrooms and a new summer kitchen. We are in the process of enlarging and modernizing our kitchen and enclosing a part of the terrace in glass for a new all year dining room. We saw an inspector one time. She measured everything and made drawings. We haven't heard from her since. Our plans are on our computer, and can change at our whim. We have projects on the list that could last another 50 years.

Croatian building techniques are completely different from the stick wall methods of the USA, so everything is a totally new experience. It is all in metric, mostly in Croatian language, and workers here expect to have a good lunch (my job). It does keep our brains and bodies active, hopefully keeping old age at bay.

"Learning a new language in our later years will fend off the Alzheimer's."

We have spent a fortune in dictionaries and grammar books, and made some of our own flashcards. Unfortunately, buying the books and putting them on a bookcase doesn't do much for learning the language. So we do spend some time off and on studying the grammar and doing exercises. American movies on television with Croatian subtitles are a great help. But just using the language is the best teacher.

John taught the Russian language to high school students 40 years ago and we both had high school Latin more than 50 years ago. There are not too many remnants left in our old heads. We had both picked up some Mexican farm worker Spanish along the way, but that just got in the way with Spanish words popping into our mouths when we didn't know the Croatian word.

Learning Croatian is more difficult than we originally thought. I convinced myself that I could just learn the vocabulary without the difficult grammar. Not if we want to be understood or understand. I am good with vocabulary and John gets the grammar, so between the two of us we usually can muddle through. Luckily for us there are many English speaking people, but they are not always around when we need them. They rightfully believe that if we are going to live here we should speak their language, so they yak away at us and we do our best to understand and speak.

We can now understand and converse on many subjects in Croatian language, but we probably sound like three year olds with grammar. Actually three year old Croatian children speak better than we do. It is humbling. Children start to learn English in the 4th grade here and many of them have private lessons before that and are anxious to practice with us.

When Drago and other workers are here, we only speak in Croatian. John has a great construction vocabulary. I have a good food vocabulary. When the family gets together the conversations are in

217

Croatian. We are certainly not fluent, nor do we understand complicated conversations. We especially cannot pick up on the very different Vis and Komiža dialects. We get various responses to our attempts to speak. Sometimes it is, "Bravo, you speak Croatian very well". Other times, the person will listen a while and then say, "Can we do this in English?" Again it is humbling.

Google translator saves hours of tedious dictionary searching. It is a miracle to us. I now have a great appreciation for how our Mexican workers felt when we spoke English to them and they tried to understand, and then went on to do something completely different than what we told them. We think we understand too, but have probably missed it more than we want to admit. Will this language experience fend off Alzheimer's? We hope so…so far, so good.

What we save in property tax in buying a place here rather than in California we can pay for our family to come every year."

Croatia doesn't have an annual property tax and we hate to think what this seaside property tax would be in California. We are saving money, right? So we offer each of our kids, spouses and grandchildren a ticket to come visit us each year, and we go to the USA periodically for family events.

The whopping sales tax of 25% takes out a hunk. Fuel is over $8 a gallon, *so stop your whining America.* Food costs are similar to the US, but we are not as tempted here to buy prepared food, so we spend less and eat better. We have a small vegetable garden with asparagus planted from seed, tomatoes, peppers, broccoli, lettuce, chard, etc. Our neighbor sells us fresh fish at a very reasonable price, and if he is grilling for himself, he cleans them and puts them on his grill for us. We have planted fruit trees and avocado trees which are producing plenty of fruit. We pay around $80 each month for the government medical system which has been quite satisfactory for us so far…as long as we have good health. There are also lots of private doctors who charge much less than US doctors.

All that our friends and family could say is "Where is Croatia? Wow, you are brave. We wouldn't even think of doing such a risky thing. ………………When can we come over?"

In the last 10 years, Croatia has become a very popular

vacation destination for Americans and Europeans. Now no one asks us "where is Croatia?"

We keep asking ourselves, "How could we be so lucky to have John's ancestors come from this paradise island?"   In retrospect, we were brave (and more than a little naïve) and the whole thing could have turned out to be a disaster. Without the dual citizenship which was possible with John's grandparent's passports, we would probably not be able to own the property and could not stay here without limitations. We have been lucky to have a Croatian family here that has accepted us and guided us when we needed help. Our experiences may not work for everyone, but for us it is *SUPER* (which translates from Croatian to English as SUPER).

When can you visit Vis? Any time.

THANK YOUS

The first and biggest thank you has to go to John's grandparents, Ivan and Katica Repanić, who had the courage and foresight to leave this beautiful island to go to America to give their descendents the opportunities that the USA offers.

Many thanks to the Repanić family on Vis for their enthusiastic welcome to us and for the wealth of information they have provided for this book.

Thank you also to the people of Vis for preserving their traditional culture and keeping the island unspoiled. Bravo!!

Without the support and understanding of our family in the USA, we would not be able to spend the time away from them and it would have been impossible to write this book. Thank you to Mom, Lori, Nick, my sister Kay and our five wonderful grandchildren.

To our friends and family who have visited us on Vis, and endured and encouraged my monthly diaries, thank you. We never tire of your visits and hope you continue to enjoy this place with us.

Last, but certainly not least important, my gratitude goes to my husband, John for sharing more than 50 years of adventures and supporting my endeavors.

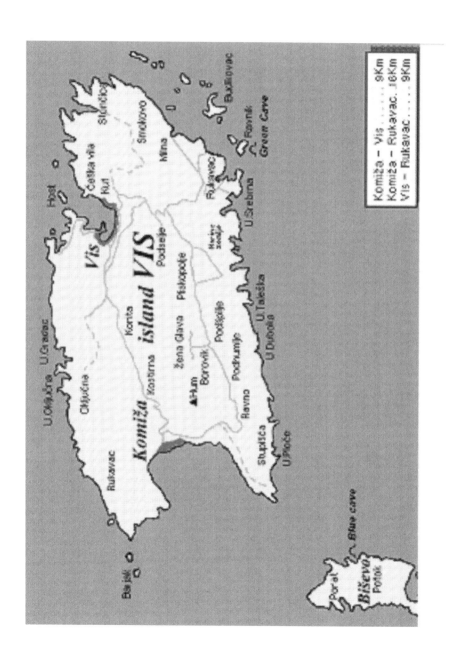

SARDENJEZ FAMILY REPANIĆ
VIS, CROATIA

ANTE REPANIĆ   1840-1912
Domina   1845-1916

Josip	1870-1920	**Ivan**	1873-1921
Jera Karuza	1875-1959	*Katica Lipanović*	1877-1951
Ante	1904-1975	Anton Repanich	1903-1972
Perina Karuza	1910-2008	*Winnie Dulcić*	1907-2002
Jerina	1937-		
		Nick Repanich	1912-2004
Josko (Jozo)	1940-2010	*Ruth Sager*	1912-1953
Ornela	1944-	Emarlyn	1934-
		Armin/Glenn	
Stjepan	1906-1966	John	1939-
Mare Marinković	1913-2007	*Patricia(author)*	1939-
Josip(Joško)	1939-		
Vedrana	1942-	Mary Repanich	1918-2005
Dinko	1942-	*Julio Maraccini*	1916-1995
Sonja	1948-	Nancy	1941-2004
Rina	1947-	Kathleen	1945-
Drago	1950-		
Lucija	1885-?	**Petar**	1894-1949
Antonio Zitko		*Luvija Vojković*	1892-1974
Jakov	1914-1979	Ante (Antonio)	1920-1994
Jakubina	1916-?	*Dobrila Borčić*	1921-2008
		Liljana	1945-
		Maja	1958-
		Dragan	1952-
Antonio	?	**Jerica**	?

Printed in Great Britain
by Amazon